CROWNED
with love and compassion

A women's devotional written with *you* in mind

Published by Straight Talk Books
P.O. Box 301, Milwaukee, WI 53201
800.661.3311 · timeofgrace.org

Cover image: Athena Grace/Lightstock

Printed in the United States of America
ISBN: 978-1-949488-27-2

Contents

Foreword

I've heard that being a woman is hard. In preparing for a recent sermon series called *God & Gender*, I asked as many women as I could, "What wouldn't I know about being a woman?" As you might guess, their answers came back both quickly and passionately! God opened my eyes to the uniquely feminine struggles of dating, family, career, safety, health, and so much more.

Those struggles are why I am so glad you've picked up this book. While no devotional book can undo all the hard parts about being a woman in a broken world, this book directs you back to the best place to find rest for your soul. A group of diverse godly women unite in these pages to fix your eyes on the one thing that truly matters—God.

I pray that you can meditate deeply on these short devotions until their truths turn into spiritual roots that produce what every woman wants—peace, joy, and love.

Happy reading and God bless!

Pastor Mike Novotny

Introduction

From an earthly standpoint, a crown is the symbol of ultimate achievement and worth. As a young girl, maybe you played fairy-tale princess or watched princess movies and dreamed of what could be. Some of you might have competed in beauty pageants where the victor wore a tiara in pride and honor. Or maybe you're a "royal watcher," one who loves to get caught up in the pomp and circumstance of royal families around the world. Oh, to wear one of those beautiful multimillion-dollar crowns for just one moment!

But King Solomon, the wisest man of the ages, would conclude, **"This too is meaningless, a chasing after the wind"** (Ecclesiastes 4:16). Those tiaras and crowning moments come from a manner of worldly glory. Meaningless and not lasting.

In Revelation 2:10, we read, **"Be faithful, even to the point of death, and I will give life as your victor's crown."** This speaks of a crown that's meaningful and eternal! We know that what we really deserve is a crown of thorns, the price for our daily sin. Thankfully, our King Jesus came to take that sin upon himself when he wore the crown of thorns to his death. Our salvation is complete. He has secured the crown of life for us. Until our last day, however, we will still have our struggles and temptations. But just as Jesus went through his crown of thorns for our sake, he will help us go through ours. In the end, how glorious it will be when we are crowned and with our King Jesus forever!

"But you are a chosen people, a royal priesthood, a holy nation, God's special possession, that you may declare the praises of him who called you out of darkness into his wonderful light" (1 Peter 2:9).

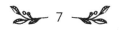

What a beautiful picture that is. Sometimes it's easy to forget in the daily pull of this world. To help you never lose sight of your new life in Christ, our prayer is that this book will serve as a companion alongside your worship, Bible study, and prayer times. It was written by women just like you who want to find their life's purpose in the Word of God—to love and serve and enjoy the company of Jesus.

Take a moment to pause and picture yourself crowned victorious by God's grace. Then read with us and pray with us . . .

I will give thanks to you
because I have been so amazingly
and miraculously made.
Your works are miraculous,
and my soul is fully aware of this.

Psalm 139:14 GW

*Reflect on the unique gifts and strengths that God's given
to you. How can you use them to serve him and others?*

_____

_____

_____

_____

_____

_____

The only name to remember

Karen Spiegelberg

I'm going to take a wild guess and say that anyone reading this has been to an event where you're given a tag that reads, "HELLO, my name is _____." You scribble your name and go about the function. You hope people will remember your name or at least pronounce it correctly. And trust me, my last name is often butchered in pronunciation!

Psychologists say that a person's name and getting it right is important to individuals. Why? The only possible reason is human ego. Recently, as I was listening to a song called "Only Jesus" by Casting Crowns, the message grabbed me. The lyrics tell of how this world tempts us to think that we need to make a name for ourselves, one that will be remembered. The refrain then points out that Jesus is the only name that needs to be remembered. It doesn't matter if people remember our names but that they remember Jesus only.

King David in Psalm 113 knew that of our God and Savior: **"Let the name of the Lord be praised, both now and forevermore. From the rising of the sun to the place where it sets, the name of the Lord is to be praised. The Lord is exalted over all the nations, his glory above the heavens"** (verses 2-4).

This world will indeed entice us to make our own names important. But remember what happens to your name tag when you leave an event. You peel it off and throw it away. That's where our own names belong—in the garbage. Jesus is the only name to remember. Let his name and his name only be praised and revered forever!

An audience of one

Christine Wentzel

"Am I now trying to win the approval of human beings, or of God? Or am I trying to please people? If I were still trying to please people, I would not be a servant of Christ" (Galatians 1:10).

Every day is a good day to reflect on the motivations behind our actions. This practice was spelled out in a public diary kept by the Rev. Dr. Stephen (Steve) A. Hayner, president emeritus of Columbia Theological Seminary, who died of cancer. In the notice of his passing, it stated that "his goal was to live always to and for an audience of One, and his hope was to live life with wide open arms and relational integrity."

On one particular day of reflection, he wrote down five questions regarding the use of his God-given time left on the earth. Was he living for an audience of One?

In work, rest, and play, he questioned:

Is this activity something where my joy intersects with what brings joy to God?

Am I living into this activity with gratitude for the opportunity given to me?

Am I able to receive the time before me as a gift?

Does this activity play into old patterns of procrastination or overwork?

How does this activity express love—for God, for each other?

It's so easy to get caught up in what we want, how we want it, and who will notice it. Reflecting on our motivation behind the activity is a great place to start living for an audience of One.

Chosen

Diana Kerr

Were your parents excited about your birth? Maybe your answer to that is an obvious *Yes*. Maybe you found out at some point growing up that you were unwanted. Maybe you don't honestly know. Maybe you've never met your father or don't remember your biological parents.

No matter your circumstance at birth and throughout your life since then, you've no doubt experienced the pain of not being chosen or wanted. Maybe one of your siblings was clearly the favorite child, maybe you watched someone else get the final spot on the varsity team or be awarded a job you wanted, or maybe you feel invisible to your own spouse sometimes. It hurts to feel unwanted. Despite those pains, and whether you were born into loving arms that were anxious to hold you or into a situation of regret or disinterest, you were and are wanted by God. Isaiah's confidence in the Lord's longing for him is a confidence you can adopt too: **"Before I was born the Lord called me; from my mother's womb he has spoken my name"** (Isaiah 49:1).

Whoa. What a cool thought! Before your parents ever laid eyes on you, before they fought over whether to name you Hannah or Abby, God knew your name and he wanted you as his. In fact, it goes back further than you think. Before God even created the very first parents, he knew you were coming someday and chose you, specifically you, for his team.

Dawning of a new day

April Cooper

What are the most astounding pleasures in life for me? Watching sunrises . . . at the beach. The sunrise is a gift. A true wonder. A reminder of a new day's journey beginning. How amazing to witness the dawning of a new day. The slow, yet fast, rise of light signifies so much.

The sun comes up every morning at the exact time it's supposed to. Think about that . . . the sun knows every day where to stand. Wow! Too many times, we think of a new sunrise as the gateway to a new day's activities, stress, or the hustle and bustle that life can give. But taking a moment to focus on the One who actually holds the sun and what the sunrise each day means can start your day off with a sense of peace and simple awe. The Lord has blessed us in so many ways that we can't even count them all. Every. Single. Day.

"From the rising of the sun to the place where it sets, the name of the LORD is to be praised" (Psalm 113:3). Instead of a new day's activities and stress, think about the sunrise leading to brand-new mercies, grace, and continued love from your Savior.

You may not be at the beach, but the sun rises and sets wherever you are. Take time to focus on the Lord's abundant blessings in your life. Make efforts to seek that which is worthy every day—all else will fall into place.

Choosing God's buffet

Janet Gehlhar

I love to eat. And I'm not limited to a meal schedule. Yeah, I know; I should eat to live and not live to eat. **"Taste and see that the Lord is good; blessed is the one who takes refuge in him"** (Psalm 34:8).

With spiritual things, I can live to eat. God's Word provides so many opportunities for nourishment, and the buffet never ends. Unfortunately, sometimes I think I'm "full" and don't make another trip to the buffet. Those are the times when I allow earthly concerns to crowd out my desire for more of what God has to offer.

My spiritual longings aren't like my physical need to eat regularly. I wonder if I felt that spiritual need as intensely, how much more time I would spend with God? When I eat chocolate chip cookies, one is never enough. I want more. Oh, if only I had that same drive for studying God's Word.

Ah yes, the struggles of my life mess with me. The thing I want to do, I don't do; but what I don't want to do, I keep doing. I want to make God a priority, but instead I allow earthly things to get in the way.

I can't do this myself. My plan is to talk to God, asking him to give me strength and a powerful longing for his buffet and the will to make my time with him a priority.

Today I'm going to feast on God's buffet.

The love dare

Tracy Hankwitz

As I study more about God, delving deeper into the Word, I see the Bible as one long love letter to me—to each of us.

How many times does he say, "I love you"? It's written with every stroke of pen. Through the books of the Old Testament when the people of Israel constantly turned from him, he said, "I have loved you."

Isn't that you and me too? Every thoughtless misstep is a slap in his face. When I insist on doing life my way, his heart hurts; yet he still loves me.

Woven through the life of Jesus, every act was done out of love. Each step to Calvary was taken with a heart full of love. And the cross was the ultimate act of love, even though my misdeeds pounded nails in his hands. He. Still. Loves. Me.

How can I not fall in love with a God who loves me like that? A God who relentlessly pursues me, who holds my bare heart, sees me, and knows me yet loves me unconditionally—no matter what I've done or how many times I've done it.

Who can say that about any earthly relationship? So, take this love dare:

Open yourself and dare to be loved like this.

Trust your heart to the One who treasures you and will never hurt you.

Open your eyes to see the blessings he lavishes on you.

Open those love letters bound within Scripture and see this truth: **"God demonstrates his own love for us in this: while we were still sinners, Christ died for us"** (Romans 5:8).

Your time and place

Erica Koester

Consider all of the unique factors in your life: your physical location, your job, your friends, your spiritual gifts, the things you're passionate about. It's interesting that when you look around, you'll find nobody who is exactly like you. God made every single one of us unique, and he placed each of us where we are for a reason.

Acts 17:25,26 reminds us that our lives are not random or meaningless: **"He himself gives everyone life and breath and everything else. From one man he made all the nations, that they should inhabit the whole earth; and he marked out their appointed times in history and the boundaries of their lands."**

Now consider all of your unique factors in the context of those verses. God has a purpose for your life! He has placed you where you are and put people in your life for a reason. He has gifted you in certain ways and put certain passions in your heart for a reason! Pray to God that he would help you see where he wants to use you.

Of course, salvation in no way hinges on our works. Rather, with deep gratitude in our hearts for what God has done for us, we joyfully manage everything he has given us! May you be reminded that God uniquely created you! May we all live our lives to his glory, in thankfulness for all he has done for us.

A powerful name, a small detail

Julie Luetke

In the Garden of Gethsemane, the evening before Jesus was crucified, the betrayer Judas lead a band of soldiers to Jesus. Jesus asked them who they were looking for. They answered, "Jesus of Nazareth."

"When Jesus said, 'I am he,' they drew back and fell to the ground" (John 18:6).

This happened so that the disciples who were with Jesus could be strengthened one last time. At no other name would a brave soldier fall to the ground upon hearing it. In the trial before the Sanhedrin and Caiaphas, Peter was listening from the courtyard, and he later wrote about Jesus' trial:

"'He committed no sin, and no deceit was found in his mouth.' When they hurled their insults at him, he did not retaliate; when he suffered, he made no threats. Instead, he entrusted himself to him who judges justly" (1 Peter 2:22,23).

Peter needed to see Jesus submit to suffering and death for our sin. Peter needed to be a witness for all time that Jesus is the true God and our Savior from all sin.

Little details recorded in Scripture are not little at all. Every detail of God's Word is recorded for a purpose. We, like Peter, need to see the soldiers falling to the ground upon hearing the name of Jesus. We also need, like Peter, to be a witness for all time that Jesus willingly suffered in our place.

Jesus is truly the King of kings and Lord of lords.

Go for the gold!

Karen Maio

I love the Olympics . . . and I hate them.

Who doesn't love watching those strong, healthy athletes with their skills and determination?

But I hate to see the inevitable fall or miss that dashes their dreams. Despite being well-trained, they became distracted from their goals.

It reminds me of my faith walk as a Christian. I long to be strong for whatever life or Satan throws at me. I am well-trained, from childhood Bible stories to my daily Bible reading. But, inevitably, I fall; sin and Satan have distracted me from my goal and taken my eyes off the prize. The apostle Paul struggled with this too: **"Forgetting what is behind and straining toward what is ahead, I press on toward the goal to win the prize for which God has called me heavenward in Christ Jesus"** (Philippians 3:13,14).

God wants us to strive for perfect trust and obedience. Yet, when we fall, God graciously gives us another chance. His Spirit promises to help all who believe in Jesus as their Savior, giving us the power we need to press on toward these goals.

So, press on; go for the gold! Remember, the only "athlete" to succeed was Jesus. His victory has become ours; and through faith in him, we will win the prize—eternal life in heaven! **"Thanks be to God! He gives us the victory through our Lord Jesus Christ"** (1 Corinthians 15:57).

And that's better than a gold medal any day!

One approachable guy!

Lori Malnes

"The virgin will conceive and give birth to a son, and they will call him Immanuel" (Matthew 1:23). The name Immanuel means "God with us."

Immanuel—God with us. What a profound and mind-boggling statement! And here's a thought—God not only became one of us, but he came as a very approachable person. Never once in the Bible does it mention someone being frightened of Jesus. He touched people, and people wanted to touch him. Children came to him, parents wanted him to bless their children, and people followed him everywhere, even inviting him into their homes. Though evil spirits were afraid of Jesus, nowhere is there even a hint of one person being afraid to come near him! Some misunderstood him, were envious of him, or mocked him. But even those who believed him to be the Messiah were not afraid to touch him—he was not too holy or too divine.

This big God, this holy God, this Creator God left his heavenly perfection and comfort and came to earth and was one of us—not as a "superior" being who was too lofty and too good for our company. No, he was (and is) that guy who's comfortable around anyone and whom anyone is comfortable being around. He never rejected anyone, nor does he reject anyone who comes to him. In fact, he wants us to come to him!

This is the Jesus I want to share with others so that they can approach him and get to know him too. God with us!

You were made for this

Talia Steinhauer

Bible trivia: *Name a book of the Bible in which God's name is never mentioned?*

Answer: *Esther.*

Crazy, right? How can an entire book of the Bible never once mention God's name? Let's take a step back and review Esther's story first.

It takes place one hundred years after the Babylonian captivity. The king of Persia decides to hold a beauty contest to find a new queen. Esther hides her Jewish identity, wins the beauty contest, and becomes his new queen. After this, the king of Persia elevates a guy named Haman to the highest position in the kingdom. Haman is arrogant and wants everyone to kneel to him, but Mordecai (Esther's uncle) refuses. So Haman talks the king into making a decree to kill all of the Jews. As the Jews deliberate on what to do, Mordecai says that if Esther is not the one to deliver them, then deliverance will come from someplace else. But then he tells Esther this:

"And who knows but that you have come to your royal position for such a time as this?" (Esther 4:14).

A common theme in the book of Esther is that God uses his imperfect people to fulfill his perfect plans and that he is present throughout.

Ask yourself, "What does God want me to be?"

Days fly by, and we often get stuck in a routine and a mundane schedule. Stop. Don't let those days get past you. Ask God for his guidance because he has a wonderfully perfect plan for your life.

Jesus calls me friend

Carolyn Webb

"I have called you friends, for everything that I learned from my Father I have made known to you" (John 15:15). The idea that Jesus is my friend inspired this poem:

"Best Friend"

There are all kinds of friends on this earth.
Friends we share a greeting with,
Meet for coffee and share events with.
Some we even dare to share ourselves with.

But friends aren't always friendly.
Some just want to use you,
Some gossip and ridicule,
Some unfairly judge you.

I have one best friend,
One that I can't ask out for coffee.
One whose face I've never seen,
Yet one who is always with me.

He listens to my fears and doubts without a judgment passing.
When I'm feeling all alone and life is just too hard,
This friend provides words of comfort:
"Be strong and don't be afraid for I am with you always."

Some will say I'm crazy,
Talking to someone I've never seen,
Waiting for answers from someone I cannot hear;
But I know that someday I will meet this friend,
Not just to say hello or share the day's events.

One day he will ask me to come live with him
And share his kingdom grand.
And in that land we'll share in joy that words cannot express.

From trash to treasure

Karen Spiegelberg

One man's trash is another man's treasure, so the saying goes. At no time does this seem more evident than on a big item trash pick-up day. You know, when your community lets you put anything at the curb and they'll haul it away! You see piles of garbage in front of homes. Then you see something else—people pulling up in their vehicles and digging through the piles. They'll pull out items that they feel are valuable to them, rescuing those things from certain destruction.

On humbled knees, that scenario reminds me of what Christ has done for me and you. He has pulled us out of the trash pile of darkness and unbelief and rescued us! In Galatians 1:3-5, Paul addresses the churches of Galatia: **"Grace and peace to you from God our Father and the Lord Jesus Christ, who gave himself for our sins to rescue us from the present evil age, according to the will of our God and Father."** The word *rescue* translated from Greek literally means, "to save from destruction." Paul was concerned that the Gentile Christians were being confused by false teachers. He didn't want them falling back into unbelief and soul destruction. In his message, he asserts his love for the young believers. Paul himself, a former persecutor of Christians, knew the beautiful grace of God, of being pulled up out of the garbage pile and rescued.

Next time your community has a big trash pick-up day, be reminded of how God has reached down with his almighty love and rescued you to be his treasure!

Destined by love

Christine Wentzel

"Before the creation of the world, he chose us through Christ to be holy and perfect in his presence" (Ephesians 1:4 GW).

Why did God go through the enormous process of creation knowing beforehand the fall of his most beautiful angel and the choice of death made by his immortal, perfect children?

One reason pops continually to the surface: love. From the beginning, God's been demonstrating perfect goodness to people, that he is the source of true love. The uncreated were created to love and be loved. God doesn't need us—he wants us. He wants to be bothered by the brokenness and restoration of us all.

Before time, he knew that because of those disobedient bites in the Garden of Eden each of us would pursue our own course, form our own desires, and die in misery forever. In our time, he supplies grace directly through his Word to teach us why we'd want to bother with him—that he turns our deaths into life everlasting.

Before time, he saw his firstborn Son's victorious work to restore all people to himself. In our time, he welcomes our repentance with his open arms of forgiveness. He enjoys a personal relationship with each of us. He's fierce in his protection of his own.

As we nestle in the safety of our Father's arms, we gratefully share this precious love story of humankind's amazing destiny through Jesus. As redeemed sinners, we can boldly reach others in need of God's love, because he already worked out the details.

Filled up

Diana Kerr

It's crazy how deeply empty a lot of people feel these days. Do you pick up on that emptiness? Do you notice it around you? You probably feel it yourself to some degree. We have so, so much that fills every piece of our lives—things that fill our closets, time, pantries, minds, attention, inboxes, garages, and on and on. Unfortunately, the more we try to fill ourselves with those things, the more empty we feel. No amount of earthly stuff can make the void go away.

We strive so hard to make our lives feel full, but the true solution requires no striving. True fullness comes from knowledge of a simple, beautiful truth. **"I pray that you, being rooted and established in love, may have power, together with all the Lord's holy people, to grasp how wide and long and high and deep is the love of Christ, and to know this love that surpasses knowledge—that you may be filled to the measure of all the fullness of God"** (Ephesians 3:17-19).

"Wide and long and high and deep." Paul's not talking about the dimensions of a boat or a garage. The message he sends is this: Christ's love is expansive enough to fill our void.

"That you may be filled to the measure of all the fullness of God." This is Paul's prayer to the Ephesian Christians, and it's my prayer for you—that you allow God, through his fullness, to make you truly full.

In your hands, Lord

Julie Luetke

Our loved ones are often out of our reach. When a child goes to day care or to kindergarten or to college, a friend is in the military, family members take a trip, or a parent enters a hospital or a care facility, we worry about them staying safe.

Car accidents, crib death, falls, disease, broken hearts, or bullying—it doesn't matter if my loved ones are in the next room or the other side of the world. I can't keep them from harm. I have no choice but to turn my family members and friends over to the only one who can protect them, Jesus. He knows where they are, who they are with, and what they are doing at every moment. They are never out of his sight.

God tells us this in Isaiah 49:16: **"See, I have engraved you on the palms of my hands; your walls are ever before me."**

God can't stop thinking of us. We're engraved on his hands, right next to the nail marks. Think of the times you've had something valuable in your pocket. You kept checking to see that it was still there, right? Jesus paid for those you love with his blood. They are of great value to him. Jesus is always checking on them.

Spend the time you're tempted to worry about the people you love in thanksgiving that the Great Protector has them not only in his sight but within his reach. As you say goodbye, whisper, "In your hands, Lord, in your hands."

Great expectations

Karen Maio

Expectations run high around the holidays: providing delicious meals, hosting fantastic parties, creating cherished family memories, and buying fabulous presents.

But sometimes the turkey is dry and the cookies are burned, and the wives at the office party gossip. Your son's family won't be able to come home for Christmas. The kettle is nice, but it's not the sweater you wanted. Flu has wiped out half the choir.

Expectations set high are generally hard to meet.

Expectations ran high in Christ's day too. Israel waited years for their Messiah, their earthly king, but only a poor baby came.

While the Israelites' expectations went unmet, we can set some great expectations for this baby and be assured they will be met. Because of Christ's life, death, and resurrection, we can expect our sins to be forgiven. **"In him we have redemption through his blood, the forgiveness of sins, in accordance with the riches of God's grace"** (Ephesians 1:7).

We can expect Jesus to return and take us to heaven. Jesus said, **"My Father's house has many rooms; if that were not so, would I have told you that I am going there to prepare a place for you? And if I go . . . I will come back and take you to be with me that you also may be where I am"** (John 14:2,3).

What comfort and joy these expectations bring!

Try to relax your secular Christmas expectations this year and focus on your sacred ones instead. Cherish the baby Jesus and the gifts he brings. Celebrate the newborn King and have a merry Christmas!

Foolishness

Carolyn Webb

One day while listening to a sermon about creation, my brain was having an argument with my soul.

Brain: This is ridiculous. You're a well-educated individual. How can you possibly believe God created everything in seven days?

Soul: Isn't believing without proof the definition of faith?

Brain: Sure, but science shows a link between species. Evolution is an accepted theory.

Soul: You did just say theory. No one has been able to recreate the "big bang." No one has been able to change a living thing from one species to another. Basically, accepting evolution is an act of faith, but in this case, it is faith in the ideas of man. Do you want to put your faith in man's ideas that are sure to change or in God's story that has remained the same for centuries?

Brain: When you put it that way, I must agree that believing the creation story is a better way to go. If I start choosing the parts of the Bible I want to believe, then all my Bible beliefs are at risk. If I don't accept God's story of creation, how can I accept God's story of salvation? **"For the message of the cross is foolishness to those who are perishing, but to us who are being saved it is the power of God"** (1 Corinthians 1:18).

Call me a fool if you want, but I'm thankful that the Holy Spirit called me to leave my wisdom behind. **"I am not ashamed of the gospel, because it is the power of God that brings salvation to everyone who believes"** (Romans 1:16).

God is within her, she will not fall; God will help her at break of day.

Psalm 46:5

Overwhelm, worry, busyness . . . What would happen if you took a few minutes to stop and think about this passage? In what moments do you need this reminder the most?

_____

_____

_____

_____

_____

_____

_____

_____

_____

Woman of the world

Christine Wentzel

When a woman of the world meets the gender/role principles of the Bible, there can be a head-on collision. As she listens to these truths, she might be nodding her head "yes," but inside she could fear surrendering everything she self-identifies with. Will she lay aside her prideful notions long enough to comprehend the good news of her priceless worth and privileged purpose in her Creator's eyes?

"There are neither Jews nor Greeks, slaves nor free people, males nor females. You are all the same in Christ Jesus" (Galatians 3:28 GW).

In this crucial time of seeking, a learned man of God can demonstrate his honed servant/leadership skills to this woman of the world by approaching her with the same grace and equity given to him by his Savior. Inspire her with gospel-driven words that feed the spark of faith in her deliverance, grow the Spirit's wisdom, and build confidence with her new walk in Christ.

If you are a woman of the world seeking your identity as a woman of God, please talk to a trusted Christian woman. Many of us have been there. Don't let your questioning cause you to run back into the arms of a dying world. Jesus is the only one who turns all cultures and authorities on their heads. Jesus made you worthy in your heavenly Father's eyes, and he intends for you to live a life of holy purpose right now and forever to his glory!

Before the storm

April Cooper

Ever planned a beach vacation and the sunny skies forecast unexpectedly changes on the day you arrive? The meteorologist gives surprising news that the blue skies you have today will soon change to a life-threatening storm that just developed over the ocean. And apparently, the storm is now rapidly on the way. Wow. Talk about change. The storm hasn't arrived yet, but you know it's coming. There's only so much you can do. How do you handle it?

Bad news doesn't always appear simply from one moment to the next. Sometimes bad news is delivered long before the challenge itself actually arrives. Finding out that your employer will have mass layoffs over the next six months or seeing that the damage done to your home by a recent hurricane is so severe the home has to be completely rebuilt with no help from the insurance company or being diagnosed with a disease that has no cure . . . are all examples of bad news before the actual challenge arrives.

Scripture says, **"Do not be anxious about anything, but in every situation, by prayer and petition, with thanksgiving, present your requests to God. And the peace of God, which transcends all understanding, will guard your hearts and your minds in Christ Jesus"** (Philippians 4:6,7). Essentially, these verses teach us that there is no need to worry. Do you see a storm on the horizon? Be confident in God. Rest in the Lord.

My worth is determined by God

Janet Gehlhar

Some days I judge myself by what I crossed off my to-do list or by what others have said about me. By that criteria, I usually come up short and feel worthless. That lie can be compounded if I dwell on it; and if not stopped, it will become how I view myself. Wow—what a slippery path from simple lie to destructive life!

The truth is that my value is determined by God alone. Psalm 139:14-16 states: **"I praise you because I am fearfully and wonderfully made; your works are wonderful, I know that full well. My frame was not hidden from you when I was made in the secret place, when I was woven together in the depths of the earth. Your eyes saw my unformed body; all the days ordained for me were written in your book before one of them came to be."**

God knew me before I was born, has a plan for my life, and is with me every step of the way. Amazing! Something created by God is special and cherished. My sense of worth just went way up.

What if you believed God's promises?

Diana Kerr

Do you believe the entire Bible? Most of us would say, "Yes. Of course." But do you really? When it comes to God's promises, do you believe and internalize them deep down in your gut?

I once heard a pastor say that most of our Bibles are missing some pieces. They're incomplete. Why? Failing to believe the promises of God is like ripping out chunks of the Bible.

We don't always believe God will never leave us or forsake us. We don't always believe God's Word will not return to him empty. We don't always believe we are forgiven. We don't always believe God cares about our insignificant problems, or even about us. We don't always believe God will work out problems for our good.

We claim to believe the Bible, but we doubt the validity of God's promises. It's not always a conscious, blatant doubt, but more so a doubt that shows itself in our worries, anxieties, frustrations, and guilt.

Joshua spoke some beautiful words about God's promises during his last days on earth that are just as true for the Israelites as they are for us today: **"You know with all your heart and soul that not one of all the good promises the Lord your God gave you has failed. Every promise has been fulfilled; not one has failed"** (Joshua 23:14).

Read that verse over and over. God has a flawless track record. We have good reason to be confident in believing his promises.

Rejoice in the Lord always?

Karen Spiegelberg

"Rejoice in the Lord always." What, are you kidding me? Ah yes, Philippians 4:4—probably one of the most misunderstood passages of the Bible.

Who wrote that anyway? It must have been someone living a pretty charmed life and without any complaint. Um . . . no. It was written by the apostle Paul as he sat shackled in a Roman prison facing execution. He didn't have much to rejoice about from an earthly standpoint. But through that passage Paul wasn't telling his readers to "be happy" always. That's where this passage is sometimes confusing. We think that to rejoice in the Lord means that we're supposed to be giddy in every situation. Your car breaks down—Praise God! Your grown child doesn't worship anymore—Hooray! A good friend has cancer—Keep it coming, Lord! No, Paul isn't telling us to rejoice in our circumstances or difficulties; he is telling us to rejoice in the Lord. It puts the focus on God and what he has done for us. Despite tough challenges, we can always find joy in our Lord. The Lord who loves us beyond measure and can work all things for our good is worthy of our rejoicing! And Paul could rejoice even in his circumstances because he knew the joy that eternal life would bring. We do too.

So, rejoice in the Lord always! And because Paul perhaps thought that our feeble human minds might not get it the first time, he adds, **"I will say it again: Rejoice!"**

Love is . . .

Carolyn Webb

What do you love? I love my husband; I love my children; I love pizza; I love walks on the beach. The English language seems rather limited when it comes to love. We use one word for so many different purposes. Love can be an emotion, a warm feeling of affection, a strong liking, a sexual act. It's a noun, and it's a verb. With so many definitions, how do we know what true love is?

This is what the Bible says about love:

"This is how we know what love is: Jesus Christ laid down his life for us. And we ought to lay down our lives for our brothers and sisters" (1 John 3:16).

"This is love for God: to keep his commands. And his commands are not burdensome" (1 John 5:3).

"And this is love: that we walk in obedience to his commands. As you have heard from the beginning, his command is that you walk in love" (2 John 1:6).

"Love is patient, love is kind" (1 Corinthians 13:4).

Clearly when the Bible talks about love, it isn't talking about emotions, physical attraction, sexuality, or simply a strong liking for something. Biblical love involves action. God loved us so much that he sacrificed his Son to restore our relationship with him as his children—no strings attached, not because we deserve it, just because he loves us. Our response to God's love is obedience to him, following Jesus' example: being patient, kind, caring, and generous regardless of whether the recipient deserves it. That is true love.

A trust without borders

Tracy Hankwitz

We cross bridges daily without a second thought, boldly crossing and confident they will support our weight. But what about the bridges in our lives? Are we confident that God will carry us across each one that we come to?

When things get really hard, when fear grips and worry takes hold, when it's hard to see any light ahead and the situation seems too big—this is when it's hard to trust, but this is when we need to trust.

Like Peter, who walked on water, we take our eyes off Jesus, see the reality of our situation with eyes too narrow, and fear fills our hearts. Aren't fear, worry, and stress testaments of a God we don't trust?

Why do we put limits on God? When he doesn't seem to be answering fervent prayers, he really is. He is telling us to **"be still before the Lord and wait patiently for him"** (Psalm 37:7).

He reaches out to catch us as we fall into the sea of uncertainty and asks us, like he did Peter, **"Why did you doubt?"** (Matthew 14:31).

Trusting without borders is a radical kind of trust. It's a daring, bold faith leaning on the One who has held us across the many bridges of yesterday. His gifts of grace and promises kept form the bridge of trust so we can walk unafraid across the bridge from today to tomorrow.

Heavenly Father, forgive me for those times when my faith has faltered. Grant me a bold, daring faith that trusts you without borders. Amen.

God's limitless forgiveness

Erica Koester

Is there something in your past that causes guilt and shame every time you think of it? Maybe it's that pet sin you always come back to. Despite prayerful repentance, you feel immense guilt and never truly feel the freedom of forgiveness.

Recently, I felt burdened about a few failures from long ago. I've prayed and repented over these missteps many times, and yet my guilty conscience reared its ugly head once again. Only this time I finally realized that my feeling guilty was just believing the lie the devil constantly feeds me: "God could never forgive this."

Of course, I'm not trying to downplay the seriousness of sin. Scripture is so clear on the fact that God hates sin and that the proper response to our sin is a sorrow-filled heart. But thankfully, it doesn't stop there! God extends his grace to the repentant sinner again and again and again. There is no sin too great. There is no limit to the number of times God will forgive you. The grace of God is so beautiful and freeing that at times, it's hard to fathom. But God's grace is true. It's true for the sin you committed years ago that still causes you guilt and shame. The grace of God far overwhelms the guilt of our sin; it is so much greater.

"Let us then approach God's throne of grace with confidence, so that we may receive mercy and find grace to help us in our time of need" (Hebrews 4:16).

A glory eclipse
Julie Luetke

Think of Jesus' glory like a lunar eclipse. In stop motion photography, each photo shows a bit more of the moon being hidden by shadow. Each event leading to the cross is like a photo of an eclipse of Jesus hiding a bit more of his glory.

Think of the glory eclipse beginning when Jesus permitted soldiers to bind his hands in Gethsemane. The mock trials, the spitting, and striking by soldiers and temple guards are all steps in the eclipse of Jesus putting his glory aside in order to save us from our sin.

The price for our sin had to be paid. The Father knows we are not capable of being perfect even for a day. So he sent his Son to be perfect for us. Jesus' death is the sacrifice that pays for sin once and for all.

"For Christ also suffered once for sins, the righteous for the unrighteous, to bring you to God" (1 Peter 3:18).

As you think about the crown of thorns, the lashes, the nails, and the mockery, remember that an eclipse is temporary. We can think of Jesus' death as the full eclipse, but the glory came back brighter than ever!

The glory was back when Jesus showed himself the victor over sin and death when he burst from the tomb. The glory is back for good!

"I am the resurrection and the life. The one who believes in me will live, even though they die; and whoever lives by believing in me will never die" (John 11:25,26).

The perfect present

Karen Maio

Christmas is over. The tree's needles are more on the carpet than on its branches. The decorations have been stripped and put back into storage. Cards and letters have been tossed, while the photos have been set aside to go into the scrapbook. The fruitcake, uneaten, is growing mold, while the cookies, eaten, are growing on the hips. Then there are the gifts: the sweater has to be returned—too big; the jeans have to go back—too small; the game has a piece missing; the toy truck is already broken. The shoes are the wrong color, the sweatshirt is the wrong brand, and the handmade ceramic chicken? *Hmm* . . . let's not even go there.

Only one Christmas present is perfect. Wrapped not in shiny red and green paper, but in swaddling clothes; not from some fancy mall or big box store, but from our heavenly Father. It's the perfect one-size-fits-all gift of our loving Savior, Jesus. He's never too big or too important to listen to our prayers. He's never too small or too weak to handle any situation. He's the only true God, and he came to redeem all people of every nation and color. Salvation is complete—there's nothing missing that we can or have to provide—and it's ours through faith in Jesus' atoning death and resurrection. How priceless!

"For God so loved the world that he gave his one and only Son, that whoever believes in him shall not perish but have eternal life" (John 3:16).

The gift that keeps on giving

Karen Spiegelberg

Most likely you've heard the phrase, "It's the gift that keeps on giving." It was first coined in the 1920s and promoted radios. The whole slogan read, "You will recognize them as the gift that keeps on giving."

Fast-forward a hundred years, and I doubt those radios are still "giving." Every earthly thing eventually wears out, becomes obsolete, or goes out of style. At Christmas, we celebrate the only gift that truly keeps on giving—the undeserved and unconditional love of God, who sent his Son to earth to bear our sins and take them to the cross assuring us of eternal life.

In return, I want to give him a life lived in gratitude, but what do I mostly give him instead? I pathetically give him my failures, my weaknesses, and my sorrows all wrapped up into one neat and unattractive package. Now *that's* a gift I bet you didn't have on your wish list this year! But that very gift is on God's wish list, *and* he wants us to give it to him. When we do, we receive his pardon, strength, and joy all wrapped up in the love of our Savior Jesus Christ—the gift that keeps on giving . . . and giving . . . and giving!

"This is love: not that we loved God, but that he loved us and sent his Son as an atoning sacrifice for our sins" (1 John 4:10).

Whose stuff is it anyway?

Diana Kerr

Various sources say 50-70 percent of Americans die without a will, which means the government decides how to divide their leftover assets. Unfortunately, this means there are an awful lot of Christians passing up an amazing chance to give back to God through an estate plan.

The Bible speaks at length about material blessings, and it's clear who they belong to. Psalm 24:1 leaves no room for doubt: **"The earth is the Lord's, and everything in it, the world, and all who live in it."** Everything that's ours belongs to our Creator, and rightfully so. We're not owners, but rather stewards. With this mind-set, we'll realize the responsibility and opportunity that come in making an estate plan for our—God's—money, even when we can't use it ourselves someday.

A Christian once told me how excited she feels when she thinks about being in heaven someday while still being able to share the gospel here on earth. How? Because her church and her favorite ministry will receive a percentage of her assets when she dies. So cool!

Take action:

1. Pray that God transforms your heart and mind to embrace stewardship joyfully.
2. If you do not yet have a will, obtain the legal advice necessary to create one.
3. If you're already set with a will, consider updating it to reflect the opportunities you have as a Christian to give a gift when you are called home someday. (It'll probably turn out to be your most generous gift ever!)

Appearances can be deceiving

Christine Wentzel

Recently there was an online news article/video in which reporters from *TIME* magazine talked to a charming and engaging female robot telemarketer. It was newsworthy because the robot telemarketer was lying. Listening to the recording of the exchange was troubling because of the blatant, scripted lies.

Near the end of the questions, one reporter asked, "Are you real?"

The robot laughed and answered, "Of course I'm a real person—we must have a bad connection."

"For false messiahs and false prophets will appear and perform great signs and wonders to deceive, if possible, even the elect. See, I have told you ahead of time" (Matthew 24:24,25).

Lying is an old trick of the devil. And just like we need to be wary of lying robot telemarketers, we need to be wary of the devil as well. He refurbishes his old tricks of deception and half-truths because they work. God warns us to stay alert. Edited stories, altered photos, and now computerized "people" help create a composite of ideologies to obscure the truth. What a perfect way to enhance this world's conviction that perception equals reality!

Now breathe; we don't go it alone. The Shepherd is guarding his flock. His flock has strength in numbers, so don't wander off. We can lead alert lives in holy peace, even among the wolves in sheep's clothing, because the Holy Spirit, our Comforter and Guide, knows it all, sees it all, and has control of it all.

Do not be afraid—do not fear

Lori Malnes

I'm a person who likes to have all my ducks in a row. I pack early for a trip; I meal plan and make my grocery list accordingly; I like math because I can find an answer; before my kids end their visit home, I plan when I'll see them again. I want to know; I need that assurance. When I don't know, my natural tendency is to worry. And worry is fear—fear of the unknown.

"So do not fear, for I am with you; do not be dismayed, for I am your God. I will strengthen you and help you; I will uphold you with my righteous right hand" (Isaiah 41:10).

How many times does the Bible tell me, "Do not be afraid" or "Do not fear"? Over 100 times! If you count the times the Bible says that but without using those exact words, the number reaches into the mid-300s! God really wants me to trust in him with every detail of my life.

Even when I don't know the outcome or have the answers, I can trust that God does. I can rest in his assurance that all will be well, and I need not fear. His ways are not my ways. He may allow struggles, challenges, hurts, and disappointments as means to bring about far greater good in my life and in others' lives than I can even imagine.

When I acknowledge his lordship over all, it makes my worry—my fear—seem foolish. Do not fear; God's got this.

What's your mission?

Carolyn Webb

Have you ever tried to write a mission statement for your life? I attended a work conference where one of the exercises was writing a personal mission statement. We were instructed to write nouns that apply to our relationships, adjectives that describe us, and actions we perform. Then we were to select a word from each category and put them together to write a mission statement. What I came up with may have been a reasonable representation of the work I did, but it felt very hollow as a life mission statement. Surely, there had to be a better way to determine my life's mission. I went to the book of Ephesians for inspiration.

In Ephesians 3:8, Paul wrote his own mission statement: **"To preach to the Gentiles the boundless riches of Christ."** Paul recognized, though, that his mission was not everyone's mission. He wrote in Ephesians 4:11, **"Christ himself gave the apostles, the prophets, the evangelists, the pastors and teachers."** We all have different roles. I'm not one of the apostles, prophets, evangelists, pastors, or teachers; but I am one of God's people being prepared for works of service.

Putting together part of Ephesians 2:10 and Ephesians 6:7, I put together a meaningful mission statement for myself: *To do works of service that God prepared in advance for me to do and to serve wholeheartedly as if serving God, not men.*

What's your mission statement?

Best Friday Ever

Talia Steinhauer

Best Friday Ever. That's what K's shirt read as she walked into the courtroom that Friday morning hand in hand with her foster mom and dad. As she hit the gavel that day wearing a pink tutu, vest, tiara, and her Best Friday Ever shirt, she made official what we had all known in our hearts for the past year and a half—the man and woman who sat on either side of her were not just her foster mom and dad; they were HER mom and dad.

"Yet to all who did receive him, to those who believed in his name, he gave the right to become children of God—children born not of natural descent, nor of human decision or a husband's will, but born of God" (John 1:12,13).

My sister mentioned after K's adoption that it made her think a lot about our adoption by God. He walked hand in hand with us and declared that he wanted us to be his children. He saw all of our flaws but wanted us anyway because of our washing through Jesus. Foster children can come with a lot of baggage from their past lives. They've seen more than any children should ever see, and their actions are the products of those experiences.

Are we not the exact same? We have a ton of baggage! Who in their right minds would want to call us their children and adopt us knowing all of the terrible things we've done? Our incredibly loving Savior, that's who.

Thanks to our Savior, now we can say that every Friday is the Best Friday Ever!

Flags of faith

Julie Luetke

Flags come in all sizes; so does faith. There are flags larger than a bedsheet. A large flag may be like the faith of a pastor or a strong Christian. We see them looking to God in every part of their lives. We also see and hear them tell others about Jesus. We grow stronger by seeing them wave with confidence in God's promises.

A small flag can get knocked out of a person's hand and fall to the ground. Our faith gets challenged and tested. If it's not held tightly, it can fall. Suppose you're nearly out of money. It's faith in God that helps you go forward calmly without worrying.

Even though you have a flag of faith, you may need to seek out a person with a larger flag to show you God's promises in the Bible. Don't hesitate; flags are made to be waved!

A flag by itself is only cloth in a particular pattern. The only flag that matters in battle is the one that is held up in victory. Jesus Christ is like that flag. His death and resurrection prove him to be the victor!

"Thanks be to God! He gives us the victory through our Lord Jesus Christ" (1 Corinthians 15:57).

The more we look to the victorious Jesus, the larger our flag of faith will grow. Rally around the Savior and wrap yourself in the furls of his love.

Celebrating fathers

Karen Maio

I have a pretty good relationship with my dad. He's a big sports guy, but I'm not, so we don't have much in common. But I'd still feel totally comfortable going to him for anything—seeking advice, babysitting, helping with just about anything, socializing, and even vacationing together. I count myself blessed to have my dad alive, relatively well, and living close by! The thing I treasure most from my dad is my heritage of faith.

"The Lord is my strength and my defense; he has become my salvation. He is my God, and I will praise him, my father's God, and I will exalt him" (Exodus 15:2).

My heart goes out to those who don't have good relationships with their dads or no longer have their fathers with them. But remember that we always have a heavenly Father. We sinners don't have much in common with a holy God, but we can feel totally comfortable—even confident—in coming to him for anything. In fact, he invites us to pray to him as **"Our Father"** (Matthew 6:9). Just as we would ask our own earthly fathers, he promises to hear and help us. He **"knows what you need even before you ask him"** (Matthew 6:8). The things we can treasure most from our heavenly Father are the gifts of faith, salvation, and our ultimate inheritance of heaven.

So, when Father's Day comes around, while you're celebrating—or remembering—dear old Dad, take a moment to celebrate your heavenly Father and count yourself blessed!

I have commanded you, "Be strong and courageous! Don't tremble or be terrified, because the LORD your God is with you wherever you go."

Joshua 1:9 GW

Are you a worrier? Do you fear the worst in most situations? What does God tell you in this passage to give you strength?

_____

_____

_____

_____

_____

_____

_____

Lord, get me through this storm!

Karen Spiegelberg

The storm literally came out of the blue. I was riding on a bike trail and was still 7 miles from home. The beautiful blue sky suddenly gave way to a huge lightning storm with torrential rains. I pedaled faster. I knew of a structure, albeit old and flimsy, where I could take cover if I could make it 4 more miles. Lightning and thunder crashed around me and pouring rain soaked me to the bone. I was scared. I finally reached my temporary refuge. As the storm raged on, I huddled and found myself audibly muttering, "Lord, get me through this storm."

Then I nervously chuckled (until the next lightning bolt made me jump again), thinking about the disciples during that boat-tossing storm on the seas. They were afraid just as I was! When the fearful disciples called upon Jesus, he arose and said, **"'You of little faith, why are you so afraid?' Then he got up and rebuked the winds and the waves, and it was completely calm"** (Matthew 8:26).

When Jesus called out the disciples for lack of faith, he sent a message to them and to us that he's with us through all of life's storms—serious illness, sudden death, or tough financial situations. Through trust in Jesus, he calms all storms. He promises.

I made it through the storm that day, but what a scaredy-cat I had been. What a scaredy-cat I often am in life's other storms too. Oh me of little faith.

Trust God completely

Janet Gehlhar

Do you believe any lies about God? I was taken aback at that question and thought, "Most certainly not!" But as I read a book titled, *Lies Women Believe and the Truth That Sets Them Free* by Nancy DeMoss, my eyes were opened. Hadn't I worried instead of trusting God completely? Didn't I sometimes feel that my life should be better than it is? Shouldn't God get rid of all my problems? Those are just a few of the lies that Satan uses to plant doubt in my mind.

"Yet I am always with you; you hold me by my right hand. You guide me with your counsel, and afterward you will take me into glory. Whom have I in heaven but you? And earth has nothing I desire besides you. My flesh and my heart may fail, but God is the strength of my heart and my portion forever" (Psalm 73:23-26).

What we believe about God is the entire foundation of how we think and act. A friend who was diagnosed with breast cancer responded, "I wonder what God wants me to learn from this." It was obvious that she didn't question why she was sick but rather, how God wanted to use this to strengthen her faith in him.

God loves us and wants what is best for us. Instead of asking, "Why me?" I now ask myself, "How does God want me to respond?" That shift in my thinking has completely changed my outlook on life.

Nobody knows

Christine Wentzel

"Nobody Knows the Trouble I've Seen" is an old African-American spiritual song that was sung in the days of slavery way before its publication in 1867. Sorrow was the slaves' intimate shadow, but hope led their footsteps.

The devil's arsenal of weapons includes the temptation into isolation, to permanently separate us from the only One who personally knows our troubles.

The writer and singers of this spiritual knew that truth well. They finished their lament with pure gospel: "Nobody knows the trouble I've seen, Glory hallelujah!" It rings out the virtues of hope-filled saints: long-suffering and patient with joyful endurance through our identity in Christ. As Jesus suffered, so do we.

"Not only so, but we also glory in our sufferings, because we know that suffering produces perseverance; perseverance, character; and character, hope. And hope does not put us to shame, because God's love has been poured out into our hearts through the Holy Spirit, who has been given to us" (Romans 5:3-5).

Repeat the rescue: God's love is poured into our hearts through the Holy Spirit! We are no longer slaves to our sufferings!

We are free to believe the lie of isolation—curling around our troubles and staring inward through our tears. Or we can look up and see our Savior's pierced hands holding ours clenched in fear. Unwind in his presence.

GLORY HALLELUJAH!

Safe in Jesus' boat

Julie Luetke

Egypt was the world powerhouse when God asked the shepherd Moses to tell its pharaoh to let go of his slaves. A terrified Moses made many excuses not to go. God held his ground; Moses was going.

God was inviting Moses into his boat, calling him to come and sail to Egypt. God was not giving a boat to Moses to go it alone. God was the captain. He was only asking Moses to be a protected crew member.

When you face a challenge, you may be terrified. Think of Jesus in a boat inviting you to join him. Maybe you're pregnant and afraid. Jesus is only asking you to be a crew member. That child is his, and he will direct you. Remember, God steers the boat.

In life, the seas can get rough. Really rough. Enter the boat. There you're not alone. Jesus is at the helm. Your feet will stay dry. You will be right beside the Captain. All decisions will be made to bless you.

Wait! Life's not always smooth sailing. Our feet do get wet. We often feel like we're drowning. But when we sail with the King of kings, we need not be afraid even in a storm. No hurricane can capsize your Captain's boat. He's not promising easy sailing. He's promising never to leave you or forsake you.

"Be strong and courageous. Do not be afraid or terrified . . . for the Lord your God goes with you; he will never leave you nor forsake you" (Deuteronomy 31:6).

Why me?

Carolyn Webb

Do you ever feel like Moses? Do you ever feel like God's called on you to do more than you're capable of doing? Maybe you're a member of a congregation with no teaching experience called upon to teach Sunday school. Perhaps you've been called upon to take care of an ailing family member. Could it be that you were just named the boss at work, but you're not bossy? It's at times like these that you might feel like Moses.

When God called Moses to lead the Israelites out of Egypt, Moses wasn't exactly enthusiastic about the idea. Instead of responding, "Here I am; send me," he basically asked, "Why me?" Moses did his best to try to talk God out of his plan.

God didn't take no for an answer, but he provided Moses with everything he needed for the task he was called to do, including an assistant (read Exodus 2-4).

The next time you feel God is asking you to do the impossible and you start to ask, "Why me?" remember that when God chose the leaders in the Bible, they were all very ordinary people. God doesn't want us to focus on what we aren't but on who he is. What words of encouragement is he providing? What undeveloped talents has God given you? Is there someone who can help you? Above all else, trust God will provide everything you need. **"Be strong and courageous. Do not be terrified; do not be discouraged, for the Lord your God will be with you wherever you go"** (Joshua 1:9).

Grace under pressure

Tracy Hankwitz

Some things are so beautiful that I can't help but stop and admire them.

Last fall a wrought iron gate caught my eye. I pulled my car over and had to get closer to take it all in. Graceful curves, chipped and rusted—to me it was beautiful. What struck me most was the contrast—strong iron shaped into gentle curves. How many years had it stood there? How many storms had it endured? Strong and yet so graceful. How hot was the fire that softened hard iron to form swooshes and swirls? Grace formed under pressure.

Long seasons of trials are made up of small moments that define us. Like fire they can refine us and make us stronger, or they can consume us and weaken our faith.

How do we respond when in the midst of everyday fires?

It's in our nature to react to life's pressures of fire with more fire, but what if we respond with what is unexpected and undeserved: grace? Each small moment is an opportunity to reflect on the undeserved love and grace God has shown us.

Amazing grace hung on a cross with arms stretched wide, hands pierced with hateful nails, beaten body weighted with the malice of a sin-filled world. Yet Jesus spoke words of love and forgiveness—ultimate grace under pressure shown by ultimate love. That catches the eye, steals the breath, and humbles the heart.

May God use whatever fire is in our moments to make us stronger and to reflect his grace. **"Be strong in the grace that is in Christ Jesus"** (2 Timothy 2:1).

Ch-ch-ch-ch-changes

Karen Maio

Sitting in the doctor's waiting room I heard, "Karen," and started to get up . . . as did two other women. We laughed at the coincidence. I figured they were most likely around 50 years old, because Karen was the fourth most popular name in the '60s. Name trends change as do hairstyles and clothing. Some people love change. For others, change causes stress; they prefer routine sameness. While I go with the flow with hair and fashion trends, my furniture hasn't moved an inch (except to clean) since the day we moved in. I tend to like routines and familiarity.

There will always be changing conditions in this life—births and deaths, hirings and firings, sickness and health, boom times and economic slumps, busy family days and quiet empty nests—and the ensuing stress that can accompany these changes. Thankfully there's one thing that will never change: our Savior God and his promises.

He's not going to let us go through changes alone: **"Never will I leave you; never will I forsake you"** (Hebrews 13:5).

His love, guidance, providence, and faithfulness are constant—even when we don't "feel" them: **"For the Lord is good and his love endures forever; his faithfulness continues through all generations"** (Psalm 100:5).

He's not going to be fickle and change his mind about who is going to be saved: **"Whoever believes and is baptized will be saved"** (Mark 16:16).

Yes, God is faithful and good . . . perfect! I wouldn't change a thing!

Jesus is there, even in the storms

Erica Koester

The account of Jesus walking on water (Matthew 14:22-36) is one of the most well-known sections in the Bible. I always assumed Jesus' purpose in taking that walk was to display his power physically as God. And while this was indeed a miraculous showcase of his power, I recently thought about this in a different light. Jesus could've calmed that entire storm with a single word. Instead, he chose to walk across the water, to make himself known to the disciples in the storm, and to calm the disciples' fear.

I love the words of Jesus recorded for us as he approaches the disciples in the middle of their crisis: **"Take courage! It is I. Don't be afraid"** (Matthew 14:27). He didn't bring life vests or a raft or any earthly help; he simply showed up. In that moment, Jesus was all they had. But he was also the only thing they needed.

This paints a beautiful picture for us as we weather life's storms. Sometimes God may in fact calm the storm. Other times the storm will rage, but Jesus is right there beside us through it all. In fact, it is often in the storms of life that we see Jesus most clearly, as we lean on him and draw near to him.

What storm are you currently facing? Sickness? A stressful job? A strained marriage? May the words of Jesus be much more powerful than your fear: "Take courage! It is I. Don't be afraid."

Where's my rose garden?

Carolyn Webb

Have you ever caught yourself thinking that God owes you a better life than this? One day while pondering the difficulties our family was facing, I thought God wasn't living up to his promise: **"Ask and it will be given to you; seek and you will find; knock and the door will be opened to you"** (Matthew 7:7). Then the lyrics of Joe South's "Rose Garden" popped into my head. In the song he sings that God never promised that our lives would always be easy with rose gardens and sunshine. There might be rain in our lives at times. The lyrics called me back to reality. God created this world to be a perfect garden, but that was ruined by Adam and Eve's actions. Now we all work hard and deal with illness, disappointment, and death. These are part of life. So what does God say about life's difficulties?

"We also glory in our sufferings, because we know that suffering produces perseverance; perseverance, character; and character, hope" (Romans 5:2-4).

"Our light and momentary troubles are achieving for us an eternal glory that far outweighs them all. So we fix our eyes not on what is seen, but on what is unseen, since what is seen is temporary, but what is unseen is eternal" (2 Corinthians 4:17,18).

The troubles of this life are only temporary. They work to bring us closer to God and prepare us for eternal glory. If this life were perfect, we would have no reason to seek God's help with anything. It's only through our struggles that we come closer to God and focus on our eternal reward.

Free from anxiety and worry

Diana Kerr

Let's talk about the Proverbs 31 woman.

I know she has a tendency to induce guilt and inadequacy. Whether you're a woman or a man, I get that you probably don't want to be held to the standard of the Proverbs 31 woman with all that she accomplishes in a given day. So rather than focusing on how well this fictitious superwoman tackles her to-do list, what if we first focused on her attitude? See, nothing that she accomplished would mean much if she went about it in a stressed-out, frantic, high-anxiety, snapping-at-her-family kind of way.

Proverbs 31:25 describes this woman's approach to life; it says, **"She can laugh at the days to come."** My self-study Bible says this means, "She is free from anxiety and worry." Whoa. How's that for a healthy attitude? How is it even possible that this ultra-busy woman is free from anxiety and worry? Did Prozac exist in Bible times?

What does it take to live free from anxiety and worry? It takes trust that God can accomplish through you what he needs to in the time that's available, even though it never seems like enough. It takes deep confidence in his promises that he's got everything under control and that no matter what happens, he is enough. It takes an eternal perspective that this life is more than to-do lists but about a God whose grace changes the way in which we approach everything we do on earth as we both work and rest to his glory.

God's got you

Lori Malnes

"I will be your God throughout your lifetime—until your hair is white with age. I made you, and I will care for you. I will carry you along and save you" (Isaiah 46:4 NLT).

This is one of my favorite verses—what a comforting promise! I read it and feel like I'm sitting on God's lap, snuggled in and so secure. No need to worry about my future, my husband's future, my mom's future, my kids' futures—we all belong to God, and he will be with each of us until our hair is white with age. He made us and will carry us along and save us. I can live my life with that childlike innocence and trusting security, knowing that my heavenly Daddy is bigger and stronger than anyone else and will take care of everything. What a different perspective that gives me! What a peace that brings!

I just want to bask in that today, repeating this verse over and over again: "I will be your God throughout your lifetime—until your hair is white with age. I made you, and I will care for you. I will carry you along and save you."

"I will be your God throughout your lifetime—until your hair is white with age. I made you, and I will care for you. I will carry you along and save you."

Thank you, Jesus! What comfort and peace you bring me! Thank you for being my Lord and my God. Thank you for being so big and so mighty! Thank you so very much!

"Let go and let God" is easier said than done

Julie Luetke

So just how do we "let go and let God"? Here is an illustration that might help.

Let's say your three-year-old comes to you with a torn strap on her backpack. She shows it to you and asks you to fix it. She goes off to play and never gives that torn strap another thought. She knows she's given the problem over to someone who loves her and is capable and happy to help. She doesn't know or concern herself with how you'll fix the problem.

That's the way we are to turn our worries over to the living God. This is the great Almighty—Father, Son, and Holy Spirit—who loves us and is capable and happy to help. Pretty simple isn't it: no headache from worrying, no irritability from the stress of the problem, and no micromanaging?

God tells us we must have faith like a little child. The little girl in the story has complete faith that you can fix her backpack. She doesn't care if you use a needle and thread to connect the torn pieces or replace the strap with a new one. You might see fit to replace the whole backpack. She trusts your methods completely. You are Mom. She has the faith of a child.

"Cast all your anxiety on him because he cares for you" (1 Peter 5:7).

So be still and know that the God who loves you and is capable to help is on the job.

Just a beautiful fall day

Talia Steinhauer

It was a beautiful fall day when I was walking across my college campus. A distressed woman came and asked me if I could help her find a shelter, specifically one for battered women and children. She proceeded to tell me how she and her husband were high school sweethearts. Her husband was going to be released from jail that day, and she was afraid that he was going to come for her.

"For the Spirit God gave us does not make us timid, but gives us power, love and self-discipline" (2 Timothy 1:7).

I gave her money for a cab, and then dug in my wallet and pulled out some Bible passages I had written down. Second Timothy 1:7 was one of them. Could that passage have been any better for both of us? She desperately needed a Spirit of power when she felt so weak and helpless. I needed a Spirit of power and love to help her in her time of great need. She graciously accepted the passage, pulled out her own Bible, and then we hugged for a long time.

Since that day, I've never found myself in such an intense situation, but I'm sure it will happen again. I pray that on that day the Holy Spirit gives me the right words, just like he did on that beautiful fall day.

As I write this, I am praying for all of you as well. That the Holy Spirit will guide you in keeping your eyes open for situations that need the love of a Christian.

It was a beautiful fall day that forever changed my life.

Borrowed trouble

Christine Wentzel

Sometimes when we're standing in the back of someone's frontline battle, we get a little squirrely wondering when it's going to be our turn on the front lines. That chance will come; Jesus says so. But he hems in that reality check with his entire being.

"I have told you these things, so that in me you may have peace. In this world you will have trouble. But take heart! I have overcome the world" (John 16:33).

In his assurance of victory, we have the green light to give our full attention to the moment at hand. We don't have to get all worked up for the coming fight when we keep busy making the most out of every minute.

To be engaged in every moment means working on similar goals such as these:

- *In worship and study, devote your attention to the Lord and rebuke all other thoughts.*
- *In work, use your skills and abilities to their fullest.*
- *In relationships, allow yourself to give undivided attention.*
- *In eating, choose healthy options for your bodily temple of God and savor every bite.*
- *In rest, fully unplug from the energy drain and allow God's peace to enter in.*
- *In play, participate, laugh, and have fun.*
- *In mourning, cry with the wounded and be present in their suffering.*

May you nurture habits that make you live in every moment. God willing, you'll stop borrowing trouble from the future and, even better, be prepared for entering the skirmish to come.

Acknowledging the power of the Spirit

Diana Kerr

I don't normally go about my day conscious of the fact that my heart is pumping, but it is. I also don't tend to journey through the day constantly aware that the Holy Spirit is dwelling within me, but he is.

Whether I pay attention to these things or not, they're happening at all times. I don't need to be conscious of my beating heart to receive the benefits it provides, but when it comes to the Holy Spirit, I'm missing out if I forget he's with me. Yes, he's by my side even when I'm not thinking about him, but when I am thinking about him, the moments of my day-to-day look very different.

Second Timothy 1:7 says that **"the Spirit God gave us does not make us timid, but gives us power, love and self-discipline."** Um, don't you want all those blessings in your corner during the day? I do.

I'm realizing more and more that God's power within me isn't as effective if I completely ignore it and try to be strong enough on my own. Ask me how good I was at avoiding stress eating or standing up to fear when I tried to accomplish them with my own strength. (Not so good.)

Acknowledging the Spirit's strength and power within me not only takes some of the pressure off of me, but it empowers me to know that I am stronger than I realize, only through him.

Plan to reflect God's glory

Christine Wentzel

There are basically two extreme types of planners: the long-ranger with Post-it Notes all over the house, car, and work; and then the fly-by-the-seat-of-your-pants type who thinks time is a magazine title.

Planning is a good and necessary thing. Better yet, God-dependent planning is a responsible and rewarding part of Christian living.

Our King's glory is so awesome that we tend to shine it only on the big plans of our lives: medical procedures, selling or buying high value items, employment, etc. Here our total dependence on his guidance is a no-brainer.

"So whether you eat or drink or whatever you do, do it all for the glory of God" (1 Corinthians 10:31).

But how about reflecting his glory on the seemingly insignificant plans in our lives? As you stand in front of a mirror, what will your wardrobe choices reflect? As you plan meals, will the food choices harm or keep your body healthy? As you plan to attend the next social gathering, will your words float on the wings of virtue or sink with the weight of dishonor? As you plan your next shopping trip, will it fit within your means? Is God's glory reflecting so brightly in these areas that you're glowing like Moses at the burning bush?

There's no time like the present to reconfigure where needed and get out those sunglasses!

Worth the effort

Diana Kerr

Take a second and think about your prayer life.

How's it going? Do you find plenty of time for daily prayer, or do you sometimes rush through a busy day and barely spend a quality moment with God?

Our lives are full of endless tasks, meetings, and activities, most of which make it on our calendars or to-do lists.

Do you schedule one-on-one meetings with God?

I know; it feels weird to plan out something as beautiful and spiritual as prayer. Prayer should just happen naturally, right?

But if it doesn't happen naturally, or if you don't intentionally make time for focused prayer, what's at stake? Many of us can attest to the fact that the strength of our prayer life often directly correlates with our emotional strength as we navigate the daily challenges of life.

Our Lord lived here on earth way before smartphones and emails, but he still knew what it was like to feel the pressure of others' demands. And yet, he knew what he had to do to make sure that even he got his "God time" in each day. **"Crowds of people came to hear him and to be healed of their sicknesses. But Jesus often withdrew to lonely places and prayed"** (Luke 5:15,16).

Even with a lot going on, Jesus intentionally fit in his alone time with God. If the benefits of prayer were worth the effort for Jesus, they are certainly worth our effort as well.

Christmas or chaos-mas?

Karen Spiegelberg

It's the most wonderful time of the year! Or is it? I haven't started my Christmas cards or my shopping, and I've got strings of lights tangled so badly I'd rather throw them out than mess with them. Maybe the Grinch had the right idea about Christmas. I think I'll go live in a cave on Mount Crumpit.

Does this sound familiar to you as you prepare for Christmas? Since many preparations fall on women, we often act more like Martha of the Bible than Mary, her sister. We get so wrapped up in the holiday chaos and expectations. That's when we need to listen to Jesus' wise words to Martha when she questioned him in frustration about her sister's lack of household help. **"'Martha, Martha,' the Lord answered, 'you are worried and upset about many things, but few things are needed—or indeed only one. Mary has chosen what is better, and it will not be taken away from her'"** (Luke 10:41,42).

There's nothing wrong with having some Martha aspect to our lives. Christmas preparations and traditions can be a lot fun and be blessings to our families. But, when we start to feel all "kerbobbled" like Cindy Lou Who, we then should stop and take time to sit at the feet of our Master by being in the Word. The one thing needed. With renewed hearts, we can see more clearly the priorities of the season and simplify the demands we place on ourselves. Then we can have a Mary Christmas!

Charm is deceptive, and beauty is fleeting; but a woman who fears the LORD is to be praised.

Proverbs 31:30

It's easy to get caught in the beauty trap and compare yourself to others. But because of Jesus, what do you know for sure about yourself?

_____

_____

_____

_____

_____

_____

_____

Beauty 101

Karen Maio

Age has never bothered me, but lately the lines around my eyes are starting to bug me. I tried a couple creams that were supposed to make them disappear, but they didn't work. Cosmetics are a $500+ billion industry. The world is obsessed with beauty!

There's nothing wrong with wanting to look nice, but we want to keep sinful vanity and pride in check. **"Do nothing out of selfish ambition or vain conceit"** (Philippians 2:3).

God says, **"Your beauty should not come from outward adornment, such as elaborate hairstyles and the wearing of gold jewelry or fine clothes. Rather, it should be that of your inner self, the unfading beauty of a gentle and quiet spirit, which is of great worth in God's sight"** (1 Peter 3:3,4).

We can still style our hair, wear our wedding bands, necklaces, and affordable "in" clothes. The point God is making is that true beauty comes from the heart. A "gentle spirit" is humble submission to the Lord and his will. It is meek—not weak or timid—but a kind and tender caring toward God and others . . . like Jesus. It is not angry, contentious, cruel, obnoxious, demanding, or self-absorbed.

Face it: **"Charm is deceptive, and beauty is fleeting; but a woman who fears the Lord is to be praised"** (Proverbs 31:30).

I'll take any recommendations for effective, affordable face creams, but I'll pray that the Spirit that lives within me would always make the fruit or gift of a gentle spirit abundant in me . . . and you as well!

I want to listen to Jesus' voice

Janet Gehlhar

I wonder what it would be like to be Moses and have God speak to me and tell me exactly what to do. Well, except I wouldn't want to go to the pharaoh and tell him to let God's people go, and I wouldn't want to step into the Red Sea. And I wouldn't want to . . . Sigh. Yeah, I guess that wouldn't be so easy after all. Moses didn't feel qualified to do what God asked of him either. And yet, isn't that the great part of it all: knowing that I can't do it but that God's plan will be carried out with his strength—not mine—and God will be glorified? My job is to follow God's direction and allow God's plan to unfold.

"My sheep listen to my voice; I know them, and they follow me" (John 10:27).

I let my mind fill up with many plans and ideas that become a swirling mess of confusion. Then I wonder why I can't hear Jesus' voice. I wish God had a special voice that blasted in my head . . . but God doesn't work like that. He gives me his Word to follow and has blessed me with Christian friends who advise me. At times I may feel a nudge from God, but I have to be really listening so I don't miss it. It's time to readjust priorities—again. Today I will focus on being still and putting my energy into listening to God's Word and seeking his direction.

Picture perfect

Carolyn Webb

Are you a good photographer? I'm not. When I take pictures, they're typically out of focus and off-center. Even with the new cameras where everything is automatic, I don't produce good pictures. Recently, I had the opportunity to view some of the most spectacular photographs I've ever seen. Every detail was crisp and the colors brilliant. The reflections on the lakes of these landscape pictures were crystal clear. The photos were so breathtaking it felt like I was seeing nature for the first time.

As I reflected on these perfect pictures and the blurry, poorly framed images produced when I take photos, a Bible verse came to mind: **"Now we see only a reflection as in a mirror; then we shall see face to face. Now I know in part; then I shall know fully, even as I am fully known"** (1 Corinthians 13:12).

Right now, what I know about God is clouded by my imperfect nature. I can only partially understand what his will is and what his plans for me are. When I meet him face-to-face, I will be able to see him clearly. I will be able to know him as completely as he knows me. I can't even begin to imagine what it will be like to see true perfection. What an amazing moment it will be to see God fully in all his splendor, to know his perfect will!

First things first

Lori Malnes (SG)

If our hearts hold bitterness toward others, we create a barrier against having a good conversation with God. Forgiving someone's trespasses against us does not mean the pain or the consequence of the wrongdoing vanishes. But by forgiving, the distraction in prayer is gone and a clear path is open to release the burden of bitterness. Then with free hearts, we can truly open up in prayer with God, sharing our hearts' joys, hurts, concerns, and requests. No barriers exist between us and God—we can truly talk and listen.

In Mark chapter 11, Jesus says, **"Have faith in God. . . . Truly I tell you, if anyone says to this mountain, 'Go, throw yourself into the sea,' and does not doubt in their heart but believes that what they say will happen, it will be done for them. Therefore I tell you, whatever you ask for in prayer, believe that you have received it, and it will be yours. And when you stand praying, if you hold anything against anyone, forgive them, so that your Father in heaven may forgive you your sins"** (verses 22-25).

Jesus tells us to examine our hearts before praying. He's says, "First things first. Before you talk to me, before you ask anything, forgive those you need to forgive."

Let us be mindful of Jesus' advice of "first things first." Before we pray, forgive those who need forgiveness. Unload any bitterness, grudges, and vengeful thinking. We need to move mountains, soften hearts, turn listening ears, have courage to plant seeds, and share the true Jesus with others. We can't afford to have any barriers in our prayers.

For the love of dandelions

Karen Spiegelberg

Early summertime brings the blossoming and growth of many types of plants in my yard. When my daughters were young, they'd pick big bouquets of bright yellow dandelions and proudly bring them to me. As any mom would do, I gushed in delight. One day, having walked through a yard full of dandelions, our oldest daughter came in the back door. Surprisingly, she held none in her little fists. I said, "Why no dandelions today?" She replied, "Because Nicky (a neighbor boy) told me they're just weeds!"

I couldn't help but think of the analogy to us, God's imperfect and weedy people. We try to look appealing and do good in God's eyes, but our attempts are futile. **"All of us have become like one who is unclean, and all of our righteous acts are like filthy rags; we all shrivel up like a leaf, and like the wind our sins sweep us away"** (Isaiah 64:6). But here's the good news—Even though we're really just weeds in the big garden of life, God picks us and proudly gathers us as his own. Thank goodness he doesn't just march on by and leave us to wither and die. We're made into a beautiful and fragrant bouquet in his sight through our Lord and Savior, Jesus Christ.

Next time you see some dandelions, I dare you to pick a bunch and display them gladly in your house! What a beautiful reminder of God's precious love for us, the weeds.

Now, hold that thought!

Julie Luetke

Imagine you have a string of perfect pearls in your pocket and you're on the way to deliver it. It's a gift to someone you love more than anyone else. You can't wait to present the pearls. Along the way, the only facilities are pit toilets, and you have no choice. But the pearls fall from your pocket and sink in the muck below. Now, just hold that thought for a moment . . .

WE are the pearls in the muck. We sink deeper and deeper with every unkind word or thought, selfish act, and lie we utter. We even began in the pit with original sin. Yet Christ was willing to come to earth to pull us out (sort of like sticking his hand in that smelly place!).

"To him who is able to keep you from stumbling and to present you before his glorious presence without fault and with great joy—to the only God our Savior be glory, majesty, power and authority, through Jesus Christ our Lord, before all ages, now and forevermore! Amen" (Jude 24-25).

I can't imagine ever getting those pearls clean enough to proudly give as a gift, yet in this verse, God says you'll be clean enough "to present you before his glorious presence without fault and with great joy." Jesus' blood washed us so clean that Jesus himself presents us to his heavenly Father with great joy. No apologies, no regret, but with joy. Wow.

Beauty before me

Tracy Hankwitz

It's happening again. I'm doing what I said I wasn't going to do—let life get way out of balance. I love what I do and don't consider it a job because I enjoy it so much, but I let it consume me and my time, especially in the spring. It's something I've struggled with for what seems too long. I even started this year with a new resolve to balance family, home, work, church. But, sigh . . .

A friend recently asked if my Lenten roses were blooming. Oh no! Had I missed the first blossoms of spring? As a self-proclaimed beauty seeker, I was mad at myself. How had my schedule become so full and my focus so narrow that I had forgotten to see? I ran out with camera in hand, hunting for beauty, and found it. There on the hillside covered in lovely blossoms and dangling downward—Lenten roses. Such a good reminder to live life slowly and take time to seek and see the beauty that's right before me and thank God for each gift.

Time is one of those gifts; and though it seems there is never enough of it, every morning I need a reminder that God has given me enough time. It's how I use it, not how it uses me. A new resolve stirs to slow and be in the moment, to balance but always seek him first, and to be tuned in to the grace shower that follows.

"Now is the time to seek the Lord, that he may come and shower righteousness upon you" (Hosea 10:12 NLT).

Humble human

Christine Wentzel

Arrogance is pretty off-putting, yet we earthlings are daily taught to believe in ourselves to the point of narcissistic nirvana. Then along comes the Maker of the universe as a humble teacher from a little nothing town to show us that sacrificial humility follows the road to paradise.

"Although he was in the form of God and equal with God, he did not take advantage of this equality. Instead, he emptied himself by taking on the form of a servant, by becoming like other humans, by having a human appearance. He humbled himself by becoming obedient to the point of death, death on a cross" (Philippians 2:6-8 GW).

The Lord of space is unaccountable to its confines, and yet he fit himself into a finite embryo. In humble obedience, he allowed false accusations, torture, and death to overtake him for a moment. Then he walked through hell with every human soul safely in his hands. In his victory, he opts to keep the physical scars of his earthly suffering on his perfect, human frame.

For those who believe this, he seals with eternal life and sends his Holy Spirit to abide in these frail bodies as our advocate against the lying accuser and guide for our faith walk. With this kind of personal, supernatural assistance, we can live with our family in Christ in faith-saving humility, not face-saving pride.

A model of obedience

Diana Kerr

Growing up, my mother was always good at nudging me out of my comfort zone. I remember one specific instance as a kid when she sent me up to the counter at McDonald's so I could sheepishly inform them, "Um, my Happy Meal didn't have a toy in it. Could I please still have a toy?" I dreaded those moments, but when Mom pushed, you obeyed.

Have you ever noticed that Jesus' first miracle resulted from his mother's urging? While at a wedding where the wine had run out, Mary approached Jesus with a classic motherly nudge. **"When the wine was gone, Jesus' mother said to him, 'They have no more wine.' 'Woman, why do you involve me?' Jesus replied, 'My hour has not yet come.' His mother said to the servants, 'Do whatever he tells you'"** (John 2:3-5).

It's almost humorous how Mary dismissed Jesus' resistance. And we know what happened next. God in human form set aside his own desire to obey his mother. In Jesus' mind, the timing wasn't ideal, yet even he was not above obedience to his mother. The Son of God did not forget that he's also the son of Mary.

You may not always agree with your parents or those whom God has placed in authority over you. You may not always be up to the task they ask you to do. But God calls you to obey them and honor them nonetheless. Often, they're blessed with a vision and understanding greater than your own.

God just blessed me in this area

Talia Steinhauer

5+5? 10-2? 3x3? Can you still rattle these answers off in your head? It's funny how you can learn your math facts at seven years old and know them for the rest of your life!

I'm a teacher, and one of my class' favorite games is Around the World, where they go head-to-head to answer math facts. One day I stopped and asked one of my students, "How are you so good at your math facts? I bet you practice a lot at home!"

He responded with, "Well, I don't actually practice my math facts; I think God just blessed me in this area."

"Just as a body, though one, has many parts, but all its many parts form one body, so it is with Christ. For we were all baptized by one Spirit so as to form one body" (1 Corinthians 12:12,13).

We are all one body of Christ. We all play important roles in this body, but how can we best fulfill our roles if we're not sure what we're supposed to be doing? If I don't know that I have the spiritual gift of evangelism, how will I ever get out and do what God wants me to do? Our spiritual gifts are truly gifts. He has gifted these incredible abilities to us so that we can further his kingdom. We aren't being arrogant; we're just doing what God has intended for us to do. We are living for him.

So the real question is, "Can you rattle off your spiritual gifts like you can rattle off your math facts?"

A long obedience

Christine Wentzel

"Fat" is a label that many of us put on ourselves without having any help from the peanut gallery of body-shamers. We can't hide our bad habits. We need to get to the root of the real problem. This insight about our faith walk may tip the scales in our favor: "It's a long obedience in the same direction."

"After fasting forty days and forty nights, [Jesus] was hungry. The tempter came to him and said, 'If you are the Son of God, tell these stones to become bread.' Jesus answered, 'It is written: "Man shall not live on bread alone, but on every word that comes from the mouth of God"'" (Matthew 4:2-4).

Jesus stayed in perfect obedience to his Father while the devil pecked at him in his hunger. It's a food temptation only the Son of God could resist. He understands our temptation of living to eat instead of eating to live.

Jesus, Son of Man, willingly made his earthly life a long obedience in the same direction for the joy of our salvation. We, in turn, follow him in thankful, willing obedience for the same reason—that's it!

Living a long obedience is not easy. However, it's a process assisted by the Holy Spirit, making the experience of becoming healthier fruitful and less stressful. This lesson is followed by many Jesus people learning to eat from the mouth of God first. Let's dine with them!

Persistent love

Karen Spiegelberg

Raise your hand if Hosea is your favorite book of the Bible! I have a feeling there aren't many hands going up. I felt the same way until recently.

In the past, I've glossed over Hosea thinking, "Whatever. Those silly Israelites. Will they never learn?" But, for a short book, Hosea packs a big punch with a beautiful reminder of God's persistent love for us. The longer God gives me on this side of heaven, the more I appreciate that type of love. Like a father has for a child. Despite our continual sin and Israel's rebellion, God exhibits patience. Oh, he shows consequences for sin as a loving parent should, but he never gives up on the people of Israel or on us.

"When Israel was a child, I loved him, and out of Egypt I called my son. But the more they were called, the more they went away from me. They sacrificed to the Baals and they burned incense to images. It was I who taught Ephraim to walk, taking them by the arms; but they did not realize it was I who healed them. I led them with cords of human kindness, with ties of love. To them I was like one who lifts a little child to the cheek, and I bent down to feed them" (Hosea 11:1-4).

Although it can be a troublesome book, give Hosea another glance and feel with me the persistent love of our amazing Father God!

Dual/duel nature

Christine Wentzel

Oh, the pain of our dual (duel!) nature on this side of heaven! Here's the conclusion to the apostle Paul's famous lament on the conflict between God and sin:

"So then, I myself in my mind am a slave to God's law, but in my sinful nature a slave to the law of sin" (Romans 7:25).

Daily our mortal bodies with their evil desires wage war against our sinless nature created by the blood of Christ. When left unchecked, that inner conflict spills over to everyone around us, which includes our relationships within our Christian family.

It's here that the devil screams with delight when we turn on each other because of wounds unhealed, power struggles, favoritism or gossiping, and lying or stealing. In reality, breaking all the Commandments! When this is seen through the eyes of a returned lost sheep in our midst, can he or she tell the difference between the conflicts in the world from the conflicts in the church? Will our behavior cause that person (or even other believers) to run again for the hills of frustration only to fall off the cliff of antipathy?

Whether we're in the middle of an open conflict or stoking the fires of resentment from old ones gone by (which, by the way, do affect our current outward behavior), let's stop in our tracks right now. Bow our heads in humble submission, and confess our sins to God our Father. Remember, we are equal in our sins, and we are equal in our redemption. No one's sin is worse than another's. No one's redemption is greater than another's.

What a donkey I am

Carolyn Webb

Donkeys are very useful animals, but they're also slow learners. They freeze when they're confused or frightened. To teach a donkey to go over obstacles, you must stand close to its head, hold it on a shorter lead, and coax it along. After much patience, love, and kindness, donkeys learn to follow their owners' voices.

Knowing this makes Jesus' ride into Jerusalem on Palm Sunday miraculous. **"'You will find a colt tied there, which no one has ever ridden.' . . . They brought it to Jesus, threw their cloaks on the colt and put Jesus on it"** (Luke 19:30,35). The colt should not have cooperated with clothes being thrown on it and a man being place on its back. But Jesus knew how to handle it. He didn't ride by using force but approached with kindness, bringing the colt's mother along for the ride.

Training a young donkey sounds an awful lot like my spiritual training. How slow I am to come to Jesus. After 50 years of learning, I'm still trying to figure some things out. Seemingly impassible obstacles pop up daily. How much patience, love, and kindness does God have to show me? How long will it be before I can rely on his Word alone? Despite these less desirable traits, there is one donkey characteristic I pray for—its incredible memory.

God, please give me a spiritual memory like a donkey that I might remember every detail of your Word. Thank you for the patience you show me when I am slow to learn like a donkey.

"Come as you are"

Erica Koester

A couple years ago, I was sitting in church behind a man who had, just a few months' prior, broken free from a decades-long addiction. We began to sing "Come as You Are" by Crowder, and I was so filled with joy as I considered the significance of the lyrics in this man's life.

The song talks about someone who is wandering and God tells that person to bring his troubles and everything to God—to come just the way he is.

This man had walked out of his addiction and straight into the arms of his Savior. God had never left his side. The joy and freedom that overflowed from this man's heart was such a testament to the redemptive work of God. It will forever be one of my favorite "church stories."

Isn't it so beautiful that God operates in this way? Consider the parables of the lost sheep (Luke 15:1-7) and the lost son (Luke 15: 11-31). God makes it abundantly clear to us that he rejoices when one of his lost children returns home. And he wants us to rejoice too!

The man or woman recovering from an addiction is welcomed in God's house with open arms. The man or woman still struggling with an addiction is welcomed too. The person with a rough past is welcomed. The pastor who wrestles with a recurring sin is welcomed. The person who screamed at his or her spouse on the drive to church is welcomed. All of us, in our sin and brokenness, are welcomed. May we rejoice with Jesus for every single soul who walks through our church doors.

The thrill of the hunt

Julie Luetke

The other day I caught myself on a treasure hunt. I was thinking of my hunt strategy and fully enjoying the planning. Fortunately, I came to my senses, stopped, and asked God to forgive me. The hunt wasn't for treasure but for a tasty bit of gossip.

A friend had been telling me about a person who was greedy in his business. She didn't give the name, but there were enough clues that with minimal digging I could figure out who it was.

How often have you been on such a hunt? Probably too often, just like me. God knows us so well that he gives us just the right words:

"Come back to your senses as you ought, and stop sinning" (1 Corinthians 15:34).

God doesn't allow for excuses or blame. I could blame my desire for gossip on my friend. But wait; I chose the thrill of the hunt. Recently I came across this 1 Corinthians verse. As I planned my hunt, God reminded me of his words to come back to my senses as I ought and stop sinning.

With so many temptations, gossip hunting is at an all-time high. We all need to ask God for help to come to our senses. The thrill of the hunt is too strong for us. If we give in, we have to fight the desire to tell someone else. Sin leads to more sin.

When I came back to my senses and asked for forgiveness, Jesus' arms were open in an "I forgive you" hug.

Mary

Karen Maio

At Christmastime, with our focus on Jesus' birth, one can't help but think about his mother, Mary.

From the gospel writer Luke, we know she was Jewish and from the lowly town of Nazareth; she was still a virgin and was engaged to a man named Joseph.

She was poor, despite being from a royal line (she and Joseph could afford only two doves instead of the usual bird and lamb for Mary's purification ceremony sacrifice [Luke 2:24]).

She was visited by an angel, declared "highly favored" by God, and would be impregnated by the Holy Spirit. (Why? We may never know, but God knew his daughter's level of trust, strength, and obedience.)

Mary was a woman of faith: **"I am the Lord's servant. . . . May your word to me be fulfilled"** (Luke 1:38).

A pregnancy before the wedding would cause harsh ridicule, disgrace Joseph and their two families, possibly cause the wedding to be called off—leaving her "tainted" goods no man would ever want—and possibly cost Mary her life since the penalty for (apparent) adultery was stoning. Yet, she agreed.

It's interesting to contemplate Mary, but she really doesn't matter much. The Christmas star attraction is Jesus and his birth. So, what should our attitude be toward her? Mary will always be honored and blessed to be the Savior's mother, but she was an ordinary sinful human needing a Savior herself. We can thank God for what he has done for our salvation through her. We can look at Mary as a fine example of simple trust and obedience, following God in faith wherever he leads.

Kiss those trophies goodbye

Diana Kerr

Do you consider yourself a nostalgic person? Do you hang on to old photos and mementos? Over the years I've kept an almost embarrassing amount of awards that I've received. I've got a bin full of trophies and plaques, a tub of medals, a box of ribbons, and multiple copies of newspapers with my name in them. I could go on, but I think I've shamed myself enough.

My collection of accolades isn't wrong, but maybe my reasoning behind it all is a little faulty. As I consider why I hold on to the past, I tell myself it's because I don't want to forget—I don't want to lose the memories. The little truth woven into that is that I want to remember how great I was. I worked so hard to achieve those accomplishments, and tossing a trophy makes me feel like that accomplishment is gone.

Whether I get rid of the trophies someday or never at all, eventually they'll be gone. All of them will—all of our literal and metaphorical trophies—our homes, our clothes, our sports memorabilia, our great bodies, our fame or success . . . God tells us in Isaiah 65:17, **"See, I will create new heavens and a new earth. The former things will not be remembered, nor will they come to mind."**

Our earthly trophies will not only be gone; they won't be memories anymore. Does that realization change the way you play the game of life?

I know the plans that I have
for you, declares the LORD.
They are plans for peace
and not disaster,
plans to give you a future
filled with hope.

Jeremiah 29:11 GW

Which word from Jeremiah 29:11 gives you the most encouragement? Which word would come in second place? Why?

_____

_____

_____

_____

_____

Keep pedaling! You can do it!

Karen Spiegelberg

In springtime, the rubber literally meets the road for young children with new bicycles. I enjoy seeing the little ones out on their shiny bikes with training wheels. Eventually, they graduate to two wheels. That's when the parents get physically involved! They run alongside as the bike wobbles down the road. They huff and puff, trying to keep up and cheering, "Keep pedaling! You can do it!" There will be joy when the child masters that bicycle, but there will also be agony in the process, including a few bumps and bruises. In either event, the parent is there with a happy hug or a boo-boo kiss.

That young child's experience reminds me of my faith journey. Thankfully, the Lord is like that caring parent running alongside me. When life's challenges are few, he whispers, **"With God all things are possible"** (Matthew 19:26). When the curves in the road throw me into uncertainty, he whispers louder, **"Trust in the Lord with all your heart and lean not on your own understanding"** (Proverbs 3:5). And a confidence in his purpose for me serves as a way to take away the pain. As I persevere in wheeling down the road of life, always attempting to live for him in thanks for what he has done for me, I hear him yelling ever so loudly, "Keep pedaling! You can do it! **'And surely I am with you always'"** (Matthew 28:20).

Control

Tracy Hankwitz

I don't think I'm a control freak, but I do like being in control sometimes. As a mom, I'm in control of my family's schedule, curfews, and the dinner menu. As a manager, I'm in control of buying and tracking merchandise and marketing.

Not being in control can be frustrating. For example, in my garden I can control which plants go where, but I can't control the rain that waters them. A few years ago, there was no rain for a long time—too long. To see the flowers, the lawn, and other plants drying up in my yard was sad. Not to mention the fields of dying crops that stretched across the country—all beyond our control.

It's hard not to ask, "Why, Lord?" or "When, Lord?"

I can't help but think of Job and how he complained after being stripped of everything, including his family. God's response was, **"Who is this that obscures my plans with words without knowledge?"** (Job 38:2).

Who are we to question God's will and purpose? Our limited minds can't possibly know the mind of God.

His purpose is divine. Each day is a blessing from him. He is present 24/7. He loves us and takes care of our every need. He knows what is best for us.

The rain came in his timing, not mine. Actually, I'm grateful that he's in control.

"The eyes of all look to you, and you give them their food at the proper time. You open your hand and satisfy the desires of every living thing" (Psalm 145:15,16).

Lord, you know

Erica Koester

I coached a women's cross country team at a Christian college. They told me about a long-standing team tradition. When a race started to get tough mentally and physically, they would simply pray, "Lord, you know." This prayer is taken from Psalm 139:1-4,23,24:

"You have searched me, LORD**, and you know me. You know when I sit and when I rise; you perceive my thoughts from afar. You discern my going out and my lying down; you are familiar with all my ways. Before a word is on my tongue you, L**ORD**, know it completely. Search me, God, and know my heart; test me and know my anxious thoughts. See if there is any offensive way in me, and lead me in the way everlasting."**

This portion of Scripture strikes such a balance of comfort and conviction. I can't help but be convicted as I consider all of my anxious thoughts and offensive ways. Those sinful thoughts and actions are a result of a tight grip on earthly desires and the tight grip that sin has on my life—the Lord knows them. However, it's so comforting to be reminded that God knows something else. He knows our hearts and knows every word before we even speak it. He knows our worries and our fears. But he doesn't just know us in our weakness; he does something about us. He leads us to know him, and he leads us to his everlasting love.

Next time you're overwhelmed, pray these three words: *Lord, you know*. Your heavenly Father fully knows you and fully loves you.

Control freak

Diana Kerr

A Christian devotion seems like a highly inappropriate place to lie, so I'll be honest with you: I like control. There, I said it. I do! I like things to go my way and to go according to my plans. Seriously though, how many people can genuinely say that they prefer to let others dictate their lives? Or that they hope any intentions for their day get thrown out the window by unexpected circumstances?

Today's world gives you lots of opportunities for control. Be honest with yourself—don't you love all your options and the ability to dictate your life according to what you think is best? These days, you can control when you have kids; when you watch your favorite TV shows; and whether you want 2%, skim, soy, almond, or coconut milk in your latte.

Honestly though, controlling everything gets exhausting. Deciding all your plans for yourself doesn't always go as well as you think it should.

Reality check: breathe a sigh of relief, because God's got an agenda for your life even if your own agenda is falling apart. Plus, his plan is way better. **"In him we were also chosen, having been predestined according to the plan of him who works out everything in conformity with the purpose of his will, in order that we . . . might be for the praise of his glory"** (Ephesians 1:11,12).

Hmm, my plans versus the plans of a God who knows everything and is working everything out for his glory? I'll take God's plans, please.

Hope for the new year

April Cooper

The beginning of a new year is guaranteed to bring perspective into focus. There's always reflection of the year gone by, as well as hope-filled anticipation of the year to come. There are usually new goals and high hopes. But what exactly is that hope for the new year based on? If it's simply on what the world has to offer, cloudy days and the absence of peace are sure to follow.

As the norms of the world's culture continue to shift, the hope we have must be based solely on truth. Scripture says: **"The reason I can still find hope is that I keep this one thing in mind: the Lord's mercy. We were not completely wiped out. His compassion is never limited. It is new every morning. His faithfulness is great. My soul can say, 'The Lord is my lot in life. That is why I find hope in him.' The Lord is good to those who wait for him, to anyone who seeks help from him. It is good to continue to hope and wait silently for the Lord to save us"** (Lamentations 3:21-26 GW).

Whether it's a new year, new month, or new day, we will recognize that God has it all under his control. He is sovereign and has gone before us; and at the same time, he walks with us. Walking with him requires us to surrender quietly our new year plans, goals, and will; lay down our expectations; and let the Lord and his sovereign Word lead the way.

Do you believe in miracles? Yes!

Talia Steinhauer

Have you ever seen the movie *Miracle*? It's the underdog story of the 1980 U.S. Olympic hockey team. The coach, Herb Brooks, fills his team with a bunch of 20-something college guys who all come from rival teams. In the semifinal game, the scrawny U.S. guys line up to face the husky Soviets, who had been playing on a team together for over ten years. But it is thanks to Coach Brooks' non-traditional coaching approach that the U.S. overcome the Soviets. I still get goose bumps every time I hear Al Michaels yell, "Do you believe in miracles? YES!"

You know what? I do believe in miracles. I own a book filled with miracles made possible by OUR SAVIOR. Turning water into wine, healing lepers, dying on a cross, and rising from the dead.

"Jesus looked at them and said, 'With man this is impossible, but not with God; all things are possible with God'" (Mark 10:27).

"For you created my inmost being; you knit me together in my mother's womb. I praise you because I am fearfully and wonderfully made; your works are wonderful, I know that full well" (Psalm 139:13,14).

Both of these passages are proof not only of God's incredible love for us, but his amazing power. Your Savior is all powerful and will stop at nothing to help and keep you. Although God may not perform miracles physically in the way he did during Bible times, he still performs a miracle of forgiveness when you hear the gospel message.

Don't ever stop believing in miracles. God continues to shape billions of people into his masterpieces—including you.

So many choices

Diana Kerr

A few years ago, researchers at Cornell University found that we make 226.7 decisions about food in a single day. I'm not sure how they came up with that number, but we humans make a lot of choices.

Often, we make choices rather unconsciously. In some cases, that's fine. I would hope you don't expend a lot of mental energy trying to decide whether to use a spoon or a fork to eat your cereal or whether to use your car's turn signals on the way to work.

However, some decisions are more important. Some of them do require at least a moment of thought. Are you going to jump in on the gossip about your boss after the meeting or make an excuse to head back to your desk? Are you going to allow an argument with your spouse to escalate or change the tone of your voice and speak gently instead?

The people of Israel made a lot of poor choices throughout Bible history. Jeremiah encouraged them to acknowledge the two paths before them and choose wisely. **"Stand at the crossroads and look; ask for the ancient paths, ask where the good way is, and walk in it"** (Jeremiah 6:16). Why? To honor God and to live in obedience, yes. But as Jeremiah continues, **"You will find rest for your souls."**

As you make hundreds of choices each day about which path to take, some may be insignificant, but others may have more serious implications. Choose your path wisely.

Why am I here?

Karen Maio

People have been pondering this question for centuries. They look within to try to figure out their goals, dreams, and purpose. But God created us, and his purpose for us is defined in his Word:

To come to faith: God our Savior **"wants all people to be saved and to come to a knowledge of the truth"** (1 Timothy 2:4).

To share our faith: **"Go and make disciples of all nations, baptizing them in the name of the Father and of the Son and of the Holy Spirit"** (Matthew 28:19).

To give glory to God: **"Whether you eat or drink or whatever you do, do it all for the glory of God"** (1 Corinthians 10:31).

So here's what we have to do to fulfill our purpose:

To come to faith: Nothing! Only the Holy Spirit works faith in our hearts. **"It is by grace you have been saved, through faith. . . . It is the gift of God"** (Ephesians 2:8).

To share our faith: **"The Spirit God gave us does not make us timid, but gives us power, love and self-discipline. So do not be ashamed of the testimony about our Lord"** (2 Timothy 1:7,8).

To give glory to God: **"I will put my Spirit in you and move you to follow my decrees and be careful to keep my laws"** (Ezekiel 36:27).

God may also lovingly grant fulfilled goals and dreams!

Beautiful day!

Karen Spiegelberg

My maternal grandmother lived to be 104! She was one of the most amazing women I've ever known. She journaled every day for many of her years. While reading her journals recently, I noticed one specifically impressive thing—most days she started by writing, "Beautiful day!" What a great attitude. Some studies even say that we may live longer with positive attitudes.

As Christians, we often need a reminder to have a better daily outlook. In Psalm 118:24, David tells us, **"This is the day the Lord has made. Let's rejoice and be glad today!"** (GW). But this passage is not just telling us to be upbeat and positive about each day. It's reminding us that every day, no matter what it brings, is a precious gift from God. Each day that we live in God's grace is a day that has been perfectly crafted by him, for his plan, and for our purpose. Embracing each day doesn't guarantee our longevity, but it does ensure that we are living as best we can for Jesus and to God's glory. After all, there's no guarantee that we will even have another day.

My grandma didn't journal in her last few years. She was getting weak and couldn't write as well. I have a feeling, though, that each precious last day the Lord gave her, the first thought on her mind was, "Beautiful day!"

My cactus pricked my heart

Julie Luetke

I watched my two-year-old grandson, Atticus, try to get a small stone turtle out of a cactus pot. He reached for the turtle and pricked his hand. He pulled his hand back, rubbed it a bit, and tried again. He quickly accepted the fact that the cactus wasn't going to give him the turtle, so he went off to other things. He showed no anger. He learned to respect the cactus and humbly submit.

If I had told Atticus that he couldn't have the turtle, he would've crossed his little arms and pouted with a lower lip protruding. He would've dug his feet into the floor for a bit of a showdown. However, he quickly realized it was for his own good to walk away.

How do I take it when God tells me no? How do you take it? Sometimes I'll try going around God. Sort of like, where there's a will there's a way. I get irritable with those near me. "My way" might involve greed or envy. I might even have a little pity party because I feel cheated.

Lord, help me respect your laws and humbly submit to your will. Remove the resentment and frustration from my heart. Lord, you know what is best. Thank you for loving me and teaching me to obey, even when I don't want to.

"Trust in the Lord with all your heart and lean not on your own understanding" (Proverbs 3:5).

Call me Martha

Carolyn Webb

In my late teen years, my future mother-in-law would occasionally call me Martha. Being named Carolyn, people often called me Carol or Caroline, but Martha was unusual. Every time I was called Martha, I immediately thought of the story of Mary and Martha recorded in Luke 10:38-42.

I always liked to think of myself as Mary. I would picture myself sitting at Jesus' feet, soaking up every word. In reality, I'm more like Martha. I worry and busy myself with many things: there's family to take care of, a house to maintain, meals to prepare, work to do. Sometimes the long to-do list gets in the way of my relationship with God. Being a Martha isn't all bad. Martha was being a good hostess to her guests. Jesus reprimanded Martha mildly only when she tried to stop Mary from listening to Jesus. Failing to see the value in spending time with Jesus was the problem, not working.

In John 12:2 it is noted, **"A dinner was given in Jesus' honor. Martha served."** Martha's role was to serve Jesus. What could be better than that? God has blessed me with the ability to get a lot of work done; I love serving other people and my Lord. I'm happy to be a Martha. I just need to remember to put "spend time with God" at the top of my to-do list. If you're a Martha too, serve the Lord with gladness and profess with her: **"I believe that you are the Messiah, the Son of God, who is to come into the world"** (John 11:27).

God is not saying, "No!"

Janet Gehlhar

When I was young, I was told that God answered prayers with yes, no, or maybe later. Made sense. Later on, a friend told me that God never said no to her prayers. Imagine my surprise! She said that instead of saying no, God said, "I have something better in mind for you." Wow. Talk about a shift in thinking! But immediately two passages came to my mind . . .

"'For I know the plans I have for you,' declares the Lord, 'plans to prosper you and not to harm you, plans to give you hope and a future'" (Jeremiah 29:11).

"'For my thoughts are not your thoughts, neither are your ways my ways,' declares the Lord. 'As the heavens are higher than the earth, so are my ways higher than your ways and my thoughts than your thoughts'" (Isaiah 55:8,9).

Well, of course, that makes perfect sense. While I was hearing a no to my plan, God was merely redirecting me to his plan—the best-for-my-soul plan.

The disappointment of not getting what I want when I want it is still there. The difference is I now trust God's plan while I wait for it to unfold.

Actively waiting

Christine Wentzel

We wait. From waiting on school tests to our final degrees, waiting on deployment orders to greeting loved ones home, waiting in doctors' offices to receiving test results—waiting on something never ends.

Our God, who keeps all promises, offers us biblical examples of those sisters in Christ who tried to speed up this process.

Sarah was a 65-year-old barren woman when God promised to make her children into a "great nation." She waited approximately 219,000 hours! Filled with fear and discouragement, she told her husband to sleep with her fertile servant. The result was infidelity, jealousy, abuse, and abandonment.

Rebekah waited 175,200 hours until her pregnancy resulted in twins. She inquired of the Lord, and he answered with divine prophecy. Her life glowed with godly trust until, in another time of waiting, she attempted to control the outcome of this prophecy by convincing her son to steal his brother's inheritance. The result was that Rebekah never saw her beloved Jacob again.

"Yet, the strength of those who wait with hope in the Lord will be renewed. They will soar on wings like eagles. They will run and won't become weary. They will walk and won't grow tired" (Isaiah 40:31 GW).

And in Psalm 23, we see the Lord patiently unfolding the process of actively waiting on us. He works to find the lost, care for the found, and fight off evil attacks until he sees us safely back in our Father's house.

Sibling rivalry

Diana Kerr

The Bible tells some intense stories of sibling rivalry. Cain and Abel, Jacob and Esau, Joseph and his brothers . . . their drama is worthy of the *Jerry Springer Show*!

Most of us have experienced sibling rivalry as well, but probably to a lesser degree. I doubt that you murdered a sibling, stole his birthright, or sold him into slavery. So what does God teach us through these stories? I think it's worth thinking about.

Do you notice a common theme? Jealousy and hurt. **"When** [Joseph's] **brothers saw that their father loved him more than any of them, they hated him and could not speak a kind word to him"** (Genesis 37:4). Joseph's brothers' hateful thoughts turned into hateful actions when he dug the dagger even deeper by telling them about his vision of them bowing down to him.

Maybe you can relate to the brothers' pain. All of us have felt slighted or less important than our siblings at one time, and it hurts.

When you're the Joseph in a situation with your siblings, show them some love and be careful what you say. It's natural to want to share the wonderful ways God is blessing you, but be careful how you do it. You might need to be gentle with the news of your pregnancy to your sister who just miscarried or your excitement about your lavish trip to Europe with your brother who's struggling to make ends meet.

Sticks and stones may break someone's bones, but words can break hearts and relationships.

Step by step

Christine Wentzel

"To this you were called, because Christ suffered for you, leaving you an example, that you should follow in his steps" (1 Peter 2:21).

Following in the footsteps of Christ is to follow the only path to everlasting life. He alone did all the work of making the way clear for us to come to our Father. Jesus teaches us by example. He knows where the curb is. He knows where the potholes are. He warns us they are there, and he comforts us as we walk in his steps. When he sees a great spot to rest, he invites us to stop and regroup with him.

Whether the path is covered in snow, slimed with slippery mud, strewn with loose rocks, or even carpeted with cool grass making it easy to stop and never leave, we need the helping hands of Jesus' family walking on this same path. They will lend a hand to help us back up, support our balance, and encourage us forward along the way.

Okay, up and at 'em! Let's start the next leg of the journey with a stanza from this hymn by Hans Brorson, "I Walk in Danger All the Way":

> *I walk with Jesus all the way;*
> *His guidance never fails me.*
> *He takes my every fear away*
> *When Satan's power assails me,*
> *And, by his footsteps led,*
> *My path I safely tread.*
> *In spite of ills that threaten may,*
> *I walk with Jesus all the way.*

Growing up to be dependent

Lori Malnes

As empty nesters, it's been neat to see our kids grow up to be adults, getting a glimpse of God's plans and purposes for them. Ever since our children were little, we've been teaching them to be independent—to feed themselves, dress themselves, tie their own shoes, make good decisions, etc. Now that they've become those independent adults, I'm so very proud and thankful for them!

Isn't it interesting how maturing in our faith is just the opposite! When we feel ourselves independent of God and going our own way, we display spiritual immaturity. However, when we realize how utterly and totally dependent we are on God—when we live our lives utterly and totally dependent on God—we display a more mature faith. Everything we do to grow in our faith is done to make us more and more dependent on God: daily Bible reading, praying continuously, exercising our faith, etc. I wonder if God is as proud of us when we become more and more dependent on him as we parents are when our children become more and more independent.

Personally, I think I'm in that teenager stage with my spiritual frontal lobe not quite fully developed and having a tendency to rebel and go my own way! I'm so very thankful God has the ultimate patience with me and helps me ride the waves of the spiritual teenage stage.

"We will no longer be infants. . . . We will grow to become in every respect the mature body of him who is the head, that is, Christ" (Ephesians 4:14,15).

God whispers

Carolyn Webb

The phone is ringing, the TV is blaring, the kids are playing loudly, and the appliances are whirring. There's so much noise all around us that it's hard to hear ourselves think, much less hear God's voice. Where do you hear God speak? First Kings 19:11-13 gives us an account of how God spoke to the prophet Elijah:

"The Lord said, 'Go out and stand on the mountain in the presence of the Lord, for the Lord is about to pass by.' Then a great and powerful wind tore the mountains apart . . . but the Lord was not in the wind. After the wind there was an earthquake, but the Lord was not in the earthquake. After the earthquake came a fire, but the Lord was not in the fire. And after the fire came a gentle whisper. When Elijah heard it, he pulled his cloak over his face."

The almighty God is fully capable of showing his power, but that's not how he speaks to us. God doesn't shout at us to get our attention. He whispers to us in his Word. God wants us to be quiet so we can hear him speak. When Jesus needed alone time with his Father, he **"withdrew by boat privately to a solitary place"** or **"went up on a mountainside by himself to pray"** (Matthew 14:13,23). You might not have the luxury of getting away from it all. Perhaps your only solitude is a five-minute shower. Take whatever quiet time you can, turn off the electronics, and turn your thoughts to God. He's waiting to whisper to you.

Me first

Julie Luetke

"Pull the mask down firmly to start the flow of oxygen. Secure your own mask before assisting others."

If you've ever flown in a large aircraft, you know exactly what I'm talking about. By helping yourself first, you're not being selfish. You're no help to others if you're blue and unconscious!

When Jesus prayed for himself in Gethsemane, God strengthened him so he could go on and complete the work of our salvation. It's sort of like securing his own mask before assisting us.

Now let's get specific:

- *A new mother needs sleep to be alert to care for her newborn; pray for sleep.*

- *A wife wants to help her depressed husband; pray for a Christian friend to call with encouragement.*

- *A college student is being pressured by her peers; pray for trust in God to make good choices.*

- *The holidays are coming, and you really don't have money for the gifts you want for your family; ask God to open your eyes to contentment and thanksgiving so you can build contentment and thankful hearts in your children.*

- *Your husband has just lost his job; pray to be washed with love for him so you can be a source of strength.*

"The eyes of the Lord are on the righteous, and his ears are attentive to their cry" (Psalm 34:15).

Pray for yourself first, and then you will be able to assist others with real solutions from God's Word.

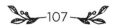

She sets about her work vigorously; her arms are strong for her tasks.

Proverbs 31:17

How do you serve others in your daily life? In what ways does your servant's attitude show your love for God?

_____

_____

_____

_____

_____

_____

_____

_____

_____

_____

_____

_____

_____

The strength of an arm

Julie Luetke

Do you have something big looming ahead of you? Perhaps you wonder how you'll ever pay off a debt, finish a degree, complete a large project at work, raise a child, lose weight, or train to run a marathon.

In the Bible, over half a million people complained to Moses for meat to eat in the desert. When Moses took the problem to God, the Lord answered with a question: **"Is the Lord's arm too short?"** (Numbers 11:23).

An arm is a symbol of strength when flexed to show a muscle. Arms are a symbol of compassion when stretched out to embrace. Arms are a symbol of power and authority when folded across the chest.

We can't come up with a problem God can't handle. God's arms are long enough to lift us out of debt, compassionate enough to embrace us through illness or heartache, and God's arms show his authority over an addiction.

Why would God bother using his arms to help you?

"Do not fear, for I have redeemed you; I have summoned you by name; you are mine. When you pass through the waters, I will be with you; and when you pass through the rivers, they will not sweep over you. When you walk through the fire, you will not be burned; the flames will not set you ablaze. For I am the Lord your God, the Holy One of Israel, your Savior" (Isaiah 43:1-3).

May you feel the strength of the Father's arms as you rest in his embrace.

He changed the world forever

Karen Spiegelberg

Chances are you will use some communication device today that was inspired by Steve Jobs, the founder and genius of Apple Inc. Most people have been a beneficiary of his gifted mind through technology in some way. At his passing, the news headlines stated, "He changed the world forever!"

The apostle Paul likely thought the same thing about Jesus as Paul sat imprisoned in Rome, penning letters to the early Christian church. Paul didn't have an extravagant device to communicate with the young believers in Ephesus or Corinth or elsewhere. He had the power of the Word, given to him through the Holy Spirit, to share the most important information that anyone could receive—full and free salvation through our Lord and Savior Jesus Christ! That is not only world changing; that is eternity changing.

Steve Jobs created and invented helpful and life-changing gadgets, the likes and complexity of which most of us cannot even fathom. But in his prayer in Ephesians 3:20,21, Paul sums up credit and glory to God for the more far-reaching importance of what Jesus did:

"Now to him who is able to do immeasurably more than all we ask or imagine, according to his power that is at work within us, to him be glory in the church and Christ Jesus throughout all generations, for ever and ever! Amen."

Jesus Christ—He *truly* changed the world forever.

God sees the big picture

Janet Gehlhar

Life gets too crazy and confusing for me sometimes. I plan out how things should go, but rarely do they work my way. I'm convinced that my effort to control my day makes God chuckle. But then I picture my brain as the size of a pebble, while God's brain is as huge as a boulder. How can I even begin to comprehend God and his plan for me? My life is like a jigsaw puzzle where I'm seeing 3 pieces and God sees all 500.

Isaiah 55:8,9 states, **"'For my thoughts are not your thoughts, neither are your ways my ways,' declares the Lord. 'As the heavens are higher than the earth, so are my ways higher than your ways and my thoughts than your thoughts.'"**

This is one of my favorite passages. When I'm overwhelmed, I read this and remember that I can't fully comprehend God's plan but I can be at peace because he sees the whole plan and is working things for my good.

Today I'm going to go with the flow and see what God has in store for me.

The KISS principle

Christine Wentzel

KISS is a backronym for "Keep It Simple Stupid." It was originated by a naval engineer in 1960. His intent was to keep key designs "stupid simple," or minimalistic. Through the years, a comma was added after the word *Simple,* making it appear to be derogatory in nature.

This simple principle can also be applied in the un-cluttered messages of Jesus' Sermon on the Mount. One in particular reads:

"All you need to say is simply 'Yes' or 'No'; anything beyond this comes from the evil one" (Matthew 5:37).

In general, women get tripped up the most with simple answers. If we can't or don't want to do it, we'll dance around the straightforward no with all sorts of fancy footwork for why we are turning down the request. If we agree to do it, but know we can't do it, we'll get tripped up down the road when the job is not done according to what's needed.

Here's Jesus' intent behind his KISS—Keep It Simple, Saint! He's telling us to speak the simple truth. Don't allow the devil to guilt you into unwarranted justifications or false promises. Instead, buckle on the belt of truth and reply with godly intent. The answers, "Yes I can!" or "I'm sorry, no I can't" will ring true in people's ears. With consistency, we will gain a reputation for being people of integrity in Christ.

When did I see you?

Carolyn Webb

A woman browsing through our rummage sale told me a story of how 20 years ago she was trick-or-treating with her toddler and infant son when her baby insisted upon being fed immediately. She said I had given her a place to sit and nurse her son. She remembered our house for 20 years because of that event and was happy to share the story with me. The whole time she was telling me the story, I kept thinking, "Have I seen you before?" This got me thinking about the Bible passages where Jesus describes judgment day.

"Then the King will say to those on his right, 'Come, you who are blessed by my Father. . . . For I was hungry and you gave me something to eat, I was thirsty and you gave me something to drink, I was a stranger and you invited me in. . . .' Then the righteous will answer him, 'Lord, when did we see you hungry and feed you, or thirsty and give you something to drink? . . .' The King will reply, 'Truly I tell you, whatever you did for one of the least of these brothers and sisters of mine, you did for me'" (Matthew 25:34-40).

Every day we come into contact with people who are in need. When we respond to those needs, it's a reflection of Jesus' love for us. The actions that Jesus lists are not heroic deeds; they are simple acts of kindness. Go forward today encouraged by Galatians 6:10: **"Therefore, as we have opportunity, let us do good to all people, especially to those who belong to the family of believers."**

Declutter

Lori Malnes

We're approaching the anniversary of finishing the big "Phase 2" of the renovations we did inside our house. Realizing this, my husband and I were reminiscing about all the stuff we got rid of in the process. So. Much. Stuff. And Dave and I are not even hoarders!

The Bible also talks about getting rid of stuff, but a different kind of "stuff."

"So get rid of every kind of evil, every kind of deception, hypocrisy, jealousy, and every kind of slander" (1 Peter 2:1 GW).

The "stuff" the Bible asks us to get rid of are things that create barriers between us and God—our own idols of bitterness, anger, hypocrisy, deceit, unkind speech—any sinful thought, word, or behavior that separates us from God. On my own, I can't rid myself of any of these things no matter how hard I try or how much willpower and self-control I muster. On my own, I'll always fail.

As a believer, however, I have God's own Spirit living inside me. He is the one who can do the heart cleanup within me. I know that when we went through our house, we found things we hadn't used in years but still had kept around. I think the same can be said of the things God asks me to get rid of in my heart. I'm reluctant to let go of my idols of bitterness, anger, etc., so I just tuck them away until they blend into my life.

Search me, O God, and know my heart. Create in me a clean heart.

Tent living

Diana Kerr

What do you want to improve about your living space? Personally, I have Pinterest boards full of ideas. If you're a dude, maybe you have a mental list of some guy projects you'd like to undertake: build a deck, put a workbench in the basement, etc.

I get sucked into the home improvement world easily. I honestly try to avoid watching HGTV, even though I adore a good episode of *Fixer Upper* as much as the next person.

The problem is that I expect too much of my home. I set the bar too high for something that 1) exists here on the soil of this earth and 2) is not going to last. I'm just setting myself up for disappointment, distraction, and even idolatry.

Scripture verses like this snap me back to reality: **"We know that if the earthly tent we live in is destroyed, we have a building from God, an eternal house in heaven, not built by human hands"** (2 Corinthians 5:1).

Did you see what word was used there? *Tent.* The Bible uses this word multiple times when talking about our homes and about our bodies. Picturing my home as nothing more than a tent majorly reduces my expectations of how great it should be and what it should provide me. It's temporary.

So who cares about earthly tents? I've got an eternal mansion waiting for me that Jesus bought for me. I'm asking for God's help to focus on that instead.

A great cloud of witnesses

Erica Koester

I can't get through Hebrews chapter 11 without getting emotional. It tells many accounts of Old Testament believers who followed God's instructions because they believed in God's promises. To name a few:

"By faith even Sarah, who was past childbearing age, was enabled to bear children because she considered him faithful who had made the promise" (verse 11).

"By faith Noah, when warned about things not yet seen, in holy fear built an ark to save his family" (verse 7).

"[Moses] **regarded disgrace for the sake of Christ as of greater value than the treasures of Egypt"** (verse 26).

And then Hebrews 12:1,2 says, **"Therefore, since we are surrounded by such a great cloud of witnesses, let us throw off everything that hinders and the sin that so easily entangles. And let us run with perseverance the race marked out for us, fixing our eyes on Jesus, the pioneer and perfecter of faith."**

Often it's the part about running with perseverance that gets placed on Christian mugs and T-shirts, but the preceding passage provides important context. The Old Testament believers are not just biblical characters; they are fellow Christians who ran their race many years before we did. They now serve as a powerful cloud of witnesses to us present-day believers. When we consider their faith in God's promises, we will be emboldened to throw off all earthly distractions and run our race with eyes fixed only on Jesus. God's promise of eternal life came true for Old Testament believers, and it awaits us at the finish line too.

Desperate lives

Christine Wentzel

"Before I formed you in the womb I knew you" (Jeremiah 1:5).

Walking through the neonatal intensive care unit of a hospital is a wonder to behold. Tiny babies as young as 23 weeks live there—17 weeks prematurely out of their mothers' wombs! They are very much alive and very much little people.

Walking through a clinic that provides abortions on demand is a benign exercise. It looks like any women's medical center, but death waits behind the leaflets with slogans such as "care, no matter what."

People are desperate to save these little lives . . . and end them.

Satan is at work when someone is contemplating abortion. He camouflages his poisonous lies with human logic that crowds a woman's mind with self-absorbed excuses about her pregnancy and motherhood: "I don't need this!" "I can't handle that!" He'll work on weak loved ones to back up her fear-filled justifications.

Thanks to the indwelling of the Holy Spirit, Christians are battle equipped, trained, and tested to help save desperate lives. Triage for these expectant mothers is the balm of understanding and compassion along with the revelation from God's own mouth about the value of all human life. We need to be well-informed on pro-life avenues.

Desperate lives need not heed the world's call for desperate measures.

Spring-cleaning the lions' den

Tracy Hankwitz

Growing up, my mom cleaned the house from top to bottom every spring. I don't know if spring-cleaning is still a thing, but I suggest you try it—with a little twist. Instead of cleaning your house, spring-clean the lions' den.

The lions' den? I recently heard a sermon on Daniel and the precarious situation he was thrown in. The pastor asked the question, "What's your lions' den?" I've been thinking about that and hope you'll ask yourself the same question.

Have you fallen into a pit of bad habits like overspending, gossiping, or skipping time with God? Have you been lured into the pit of worldly delights like immorality on the internet? Maybe it's the pit of selfishness, doing whatever pleases you, or the pits we actually jump into—the pits of temptation and secret sins.

These may not seem like lions' dens, but don't be fooled—the lions are waiting in the darkness. **"Your enemy the devil prowls around like a roaring lion looking for someone to devour"** (1 Peter 5:8). The devil plays mind games, but the fight for your soul is no game. Each one of our wrongdoings is weighing us down, pulling us further into that pit. Only God can save us.

So open the windows and air out the closets of your heart. Expose those dark corners to God's light of truth, and he will scrub them clean with forgiveness. Being vulnerable and honest is scary, but remember that God loves you and his mercies are new every morning.

I need a vacation

Carolyn Webb

I need a vacation! I'm sure that at some point you really needed to get away from the troubles and stresses in your life. That's what vacation is all about. Whether you have a staycation or travel somewhere exciting, it feels good to take a break.

Jesus also recognized the need for vacation. When his disciples were overwhelmed **"because so many people were coming and going that they did not even have a chance to eat, [Jesus] said to them, 'Come with me by yourselves to a quiet place and get some rest.' So they went away by themselves in a boat to a solitary place"** (Mark 6:31,32). The Bible also tells us **"Jesus often withdrew to lonely places and prayed"** (Luke 5:16). These mini-vacations allowed him to renew mind, body and, most important, spirit. When Jesus took a break from work, his primary purpose was to spend time with his Father in prayer. When he returned from his time away, Jesus was ready to resume his work of preaching the good news of the kingdom of God.

Vacations are an important part of life. These breaks allow us to recharge and return to our work with new energy. Whether you're planning an extravagant trip or simply a break away from the usual routine, include some quality time with your heavenly family. Remember Jesus' invitation and promise: **"Come to me, all you who are weary and burdened, and I will give you rest"** (Matthew 11:28).

Clickbait

Christine Wentzel

Clickbait are social networking headlines written to grab our attention. They range from legitimate news sources to sensationalized gossip rags.

We're living in a damaged world with damaged intentions. It conditions us to jump to conclusions easily and quickly. If the bait is enticing enough, once clicked, it will take us to multiple layers of rewrites laden with personal biases along the way. By the time we reach the end, the facts no longer match the headline. How many of us bother to dig to the original source? We're conditioned to be lazy information gatherers who slide into breaking the Lord's commandment against lying about our neighbors.

That's the intention of most of these clickbait headlines, to harm our neighbor's name and reputation. Who is our neighbor? Everyone.

"Never lie when you testify about your neighbor" (Exodus 20:16 GW).

It doesn't affect us much unless we consider people close to our hearts. Consider this headline:

TWO RELIGIOUS MEN ENTER HOUSE OF PROSTITUTE—SLINK OUT THE BACK WINDOW!

If you stop there, you'd miss the fact that the prostitute, Rahab, an ancestor of Jesus, was protecting the spies Joshua sent to check out the Promised Land.

Let's practice godly discernment and give people the benefit of the doubt. Be aware that for every link we click, the network is wired to send us more like it. We can slow down the toxic newsfeed.

Great expectations

Diana Kerr

It's almost comical how perceptive women are to their husbands' flaws. "You really shouldn't eat that. You're getting a beer belly, and you haven't worked out in weeks." A patient husband might accept the nagging, while another might not be afraid to point out that his wife isn't exactly the same size she was on their wedding day either.

It's too bad we're so good at holding others to higher standards than our own. We expect better behavior from spouses, children, siblings, coworkers, friends, and pastors than we expect of ourselves. When they don't live up to our expectations, we sometimes even call them out.

We're not the only ones suffering from this hypocrisy disease. After King David killed off his mistress' husband, the prophet Nathan visited him and told him a story. The fictional story was of a wealthy man who killed another man's only lamb. David failed to see that the story referred to him, and his response was all too familiar to our own in this type of situation: **"David burned with anger against the man and said to Nathan, 'As surely as the LORD lives, the man who did this must die! He must pay for that lamb four times over, because he did such a thing and had no pity'"** (2 Samuel 12:5,6). Ouch. Wrong answer, David.

Thanks to Nathan, David eventually learned his lesson, and it's a lesson for us too: don't set the bar so high for others when you can't even make it over the bar yourself.

You'll never believe #4!

Talia Steinhauer

Okay, it's time to confess that I have a weakness for *BuzzFeed* articles. It's not that I really want to know what the ten reasons for "whatever doesn't matter" are, but it's the fact that I really just have to know! I have to know what #4 is, even though it always ends up being disappointing. Just a word of advice: #4 is never as cool as they say it is.

"May the God of hope fill you with all joy and peace as you trust in him, so that you may overflow with hope by the power of the Holy Spirit" (Romans 15:13).

Do you ever get caught up in the worldly thinking that we need a reason to be joyful? Do you ever feel like you're constantly searching for the next best thing to make you happy? Read Romans 15:13 a few times. What sticks out to you? Are you currently overflowing with hope? Do the people around you notice how you overflow because of your absolute trust in God and because of the power of the Holy Spirit?

Imagine if God were a *BuzzFeed* article: "10 Reasons Why You Should Be Joyful—You'll Never Believe #4!"

#4. God sent his one and only Son to die on a cross for your selfish and sinful self!

Open your Bible today with #4 in mind. Open your Bible with the excitement that its contents won't disappoint you like an article but will fill you up so much that you'll overflow with joy!

Lasting impressions
Christine Wentzel

"How much do you have to hate someone to believe everlasting life is possible and not tell them that?"

This bold statement was made by atheist/entertainer Penn Jilette of Penn & Teller magic fame. In a video I watched recently, Penn recalled an encounter with an audience member who participated in one of their stage acts the night before. This man returned the next night and waited with a group of fans to get autographs. He brought along the props given to him after his bit with them and a small Bible.

Penn makes his living off of fakery, so it's revealing how he described this man in his short video clip: complimentary, kind, nice, sane, wonderful, not defensive, made eye contact, good guy, polite, honest, cared enough to proselytize, gave him a Bible.

"Therefore, since we have such a hope, we are very bold. But whenever anyone turns to the Lord, the veil is taken away" (2 Corinthians 3:12,16).

This man made a lasting impression on Penn. The guy looked Penn in the eyes and handed him a pocket Bible with all his contact information written in it. By most, he would be shrugged off as one of those kooky Bible thumpers, but it was his Christ-like honesty that made the difference. Penn recognized the face of Jesus, even though he didn't believe it. The rest is up to God.

A simple crossword puzzle

Julie Luetke

I stumbled on to a little paperback that turned out to be quite an eye-opener. It was just a simple crossword puzzle book. The book was full of Bible puzzles. As I did the puzzle on Jonah, I was pulled to the pages of my Bible for a few of the answers. Instantly, I was reminded how much I love God's Word. A simple crossword puzzle meant for children brought me back where I belong. One question took me to the prayer Jonah prayed from inside the fish. Here are some excerpts from it in Jonah chapter 2:

- **"In my distress I called to the LORD and he answered me."**

- **"You, LORD my God, brought my life up from the pit."**

- **"Those who cling to worthless idols turn away from God's love for them."**

- **"Salvation comes from the LORD."**

It's easy to fill our days with things that can waste our time like puzzles or browsing the internet. Spending time in God's Word feeds our faith and brings us closer to God. If making time to read the Bible is hard, try an audio version while you go walking or have someone read to you while you clean up the kitchen. Listening to Bible stories read by your children will leave a lasting impression on them. Having your husband read to you will bind a marriage. Maybe you need to get a Bible crossword puzzle book.

It was just a simple crossword puzzle, but it took me back where I needed to be. Thank you, Jesus.

Keep your eyes open

Karen Maio

Sometimes people are just oblivious. (My husband once told me he was driving next to my car all the way to my exit. I need to keep my eyes open all around me!) Sometimes people are too focused on a single task. (Have you ever seen somebody using a smartphone walk into something? While it's kind of funny, the fact remains that that person needs to be looking up and around.)

We need to keep our eyes open, not just for our and others' safety, but for something even more important.

Jesus' disciples were a little oblivious at times. Jesus often spoke using word pictures: **"I have food to eat that you know nothing about."** To which the clueless disciples replied, **"Could someone have brought him food?"** Jesus explained, **"'My food,' said Jesus, 'is to do the will of him who sent me and to finish his work. . . . Open your eyes and look at the fields! They are ripe for harvest'"** (John 4:32-35).

This is the real reason we need to keep our eyes open. There are people all around us who are hurting or oblivious and need the Lord! If we are too busy or self-absorbed, we may miss the clues and opportunities to offer an encouraging word or Bible passage, lend a helping hand, or start a conversation that could ultimately lead them to know about the Lord's saving grace. Sharing our faith is one of the reasons why we exist, so pay attention and look for opportunities. Keep your eyes open!

Gossip—who me?

Karen Spiegelberg

Psst . . . did you hear . . . did you hear that gossip is deadly? What?! Proverbs 11:9 tells us, **"With their mouths the godless destroy their neighbors."** Paul, in his letter to the Romans, is even tougher in his words: **"Although they know God's righteous decree that those who do such things deserve death, they not only continue to do these very things but also approve of those who practice them"** (1:32). Deserve death? That really caught my attention and had me scrambling for a definition of *gossip*. Gossip is any communication that hurts people, reveals a secret, or challenges someone's character.

So why do we gossip? We gossip because our broken nature loves the lure of good, juicy information. And what is the source of these actions? Satan. Satan started gossip. Jesus Christ, in John 8:44 said, **"He was a murderer from the beginning."** Today Satan uses us as his conduits. It sounds something like this: "Just between you and me . . ." or "You might want to keep 'so and so' in your prayers because . . ."

God hates gossip! I'm shocked at how many Bible passages reference gossip. This should tip us off at the seriousness of it. With God's help and forgiveness, we can turn this behavior around.

Next time gossip becomes alluring, draw on this passage: **"Do not let any unwholesome talk come out of your mouths, but only what is helpful for building others up"** (Ephesians 4:29). Tattoo it on your arm if necessary! I just might.

The LORD will fight for you; you need only to be still.

Exodus 14:14

*Oh, to be still! It's easier said than done, isn't it?
In what ways can you practice setting aside your
worry and being still and content, knowing that
God's got your back in all situations?*

_____

_____

_____

_____

_____

_____

_____

_____

On God's wing

Karen Spiegelberg

It was a glorious morning in northern Wisconsin where my husband, daughters, and I were vacationing on a lake. As I sipped coffee in peace, I noticed an eagle soaring from a nest in a tall pine tree. Then I saw a baby eagle tumble out of the nest and try desperately to flutter into flight. It plunged downward toward the lake! I gasped, but then the mama eagle swooped back and rescued her offspring with one wing, raising it back up to the nest. It was one of the coolest things I've ever seen.

What a fabulous picture of what our God does for us. The whole scene brought to life for me the words of the song "On Eagle's Wings" (written by Michael Joncas and based on Psalm 91). In that psalm, we read, **"Whoever dwells in the shelter of the Most High will rest in the shadow of the Almighty. I will say of the Lord, 'He is my refuge. . . . My God, in whom I trust'"** (verses 1,2). That baby eagle is like us trying so hard to be strong in our life's flight. Thankfully, when we are weak and fall short daily, God swoops in and saves us with his strength and raises us up again on his wing.

God's "wing" must be getting tired of rescuing me, but I'm sure glad he continues to do so! He is my refuge; in him I trust.

Enough

Diana Kerr

I know we much prefer to sweep these under the rug, but I want you to think about your worries and fears. Think about the what-ifs, the worst-case scenarios, the things that feel like they would be the end of the world if they happened to you.

Infertility. Life-changing illness. Job loss. A cheating spouse.

Those things would be tough. So tough. And if I wasn't a Christian, I'd be terrified at the thought of those things.

But you and I are different. In the midst of our pain, the God whose blood was enough to redeem us is also a God who is enough to comfort us, enough to bring us peace and joy, enough to help us get through each day. See, at the root of our fears and worries is often an unconscious belief that God isn't enough, that if you lost one of the most important things in your life you couldn't get through it. But God is enough.

I hear God's words to Paul in my head in my moments of struggle or worry: **"My grace is sufficient for you, for my power is made perfect in weakness"** (2 Corinthians 12:9). When I'm feeling weak or fearful, I whisper or pray, "God, you are enough. I know you are enough." I do this over and over, reminding myself of how his power shines in my weakest moment and that, no matter what, he is sufficient and I'll be okay and my place in heaven is secure.

Making it stronger

Julie Luetke

When you tie a knot in a piece of string, you give it a tug. Not to break it but to make it tight and strong. If the knot were left loose, it could come undone. Pulling on the knot is testing it. A woman in Matthew chapter 15 was having her faith tested in a similar way.

The woman came calling after Jesus to heal her daughter, who suffered from demon possession. Jesus first seemed to ignore her. When she kept crying after him, Jesus said to her face that he had come for the lost sheep of Israel and it was not right to give the children's bread to the dogs. Jesus implied she was only a dog that was unworthy of his help. Wow, what a discouraging comment from the God of love!

Jesus had every intention of healing her daughter, but he gave the woman's faith a hard tug by acting like he did not care to help her. She didn't waver. The woman continued to plead for her child. She told Jesus that even the dogs lick the crumbs that fall from the master's table. Her faith was so strong that she knew only a crumb of God's goodness would be enough.

Happily, Jesus turned to her and said, **"Woman, you have great faith! Your request is granted"** (Matthew 15:28).

That hard tug on her faith did not destroy it but made it even stronger. When you feel your faith is being tested beyond what you can bear, remember the woman who came begging for her child. Remember Jesus was testing her faith to make it strong.

Rest

Karen Maio

It's a wonderful feeling to wake fully refreshed from a good night's sleep. One feels positive, energetic, and ready to meet the day. On the other hand, nights spent tossing and turning can leave one feeling stiff, exhausted, and grumpy.

Compare this with a Christian's faith walk. On one hand, there is God's rest—an eternity of refreshment, perfect peace, and joy. On the other hand, there's hell—an eternity of darkness and fiery torment. Those who hear the gospel message of Jesus and the salvation he attained for us and receive it with believing hearts will enter God's rest. Those who hear the gospel and do not believe will enter hell. **"For we also have had the good news proclaimed to us, just as they** [Israel] **did; but the message they heard was of no value to them, because they did not share the faith of those who obeyed** [believed]**. Now we who have believed enter that rest"** (Hebrews 4:2,3).

Get closer to God's gospel; stay in the Word. It is **"alive and active"** (Hebrews 4:12) and has the power to strengthen our faith. It also empowers us to obey God's commands out of love and thanks for all that he has done for us through Jesus.

Enjoy the rest you have from God right now—the forgiveness of sins, peace with God, and the sure hope of heaven—and look forward to an eternity of rest in our Savior's presence!

Peer pressure

Christine Wentzel

"Nebuchadnezzar said, 'Praise the God of Shadrach, Meshach, and Abednego. He sent his angel and saved his servants, who trusted him. They disobeyed the king and risked their lives so that they would not have to honor or worship any god except their own God'" (Daniel 3:28 GW).

Peers say we deserve to have our way. PRESSURE

Peers say premarital sex is normal. PRESSURE

Peers say getting high is fun. PRESSURE

Peers say pornography isn't infidelity. PRESSURE

Peers say cohabiting single seniors save their benefits. PRESSURE

Peer pressure messes with our God-direction and tries to push us into a corner. It's why we can't go it alone. Friends don't pressure friends to go against their principles. Jesus is our personal friend. He teaches us the worth of being in a Christian community where we build one another up through his Holy Word for heaven's sake!

When we're tempted to go with the flow to save face or justify our own sinful choices, let's learn from those who faced their own peer pressure and overcame because of Jesus. If he can melt the heart of an evil king by preventing his friends from burning up, then he can protect and sustain us through our testing.

Shaken-up comforts

Diana Kerr

We all like comfort and routine to a degree. Even adventurous, spontaneous folks like some degree of predictability or consistency in certain areas of life.

With my hand raised in embarrassed admission, I'll admit that I like comfort, routine, and predictability a lot. I idolize an easy life, a life within my control that goes my way. I even prefer the comfort of my own sin to trying to deal with it.

But that's not how my God wants me to operate.

In the course of my life, he's rattled me from my comfort and sin and he's shaken up my plans much more than I ever wanted. Same for you too?

Most times, I found myself clinging to the security blanket of my previous life. There's risk and unease in the new and unknown. Frankly, we don't always believe God's big enough to handle it.

I see my own mistrust mirrored in the Israelites' cries to Moses: **"Didn't we say to you in Egypt, 'Leave us alone! Let us go on serving the Egyptians'? It would have been better for us to serve the Egyptians than to die in the desert!"** (Exodus 14:12).

Like the Israelites, we don't know the ending of God's story for us. But the God who is powerful enough to free and protect the Israelites is the same God who watches over you in times of change and discomfort. He is enough, and he offers more than our old comforts ever could.

Poisoned perception

Christine Wentzel

Everyone is drawn to a juicy story about someone else. It puffs up the curiosity in all of us. While we listen to the latest gossip, a poisoned perception develops about the person that, innocent or not, forever stains our knowledge about him or her. To be sure, these dangerous word daggers are pitched at us when our backs are turned as well.

Satan scopes for the choicest fields to stir up trouble between people; those ripe grounds where we live, work, play, and worship. We, who call on Jesus' name above all names, are his prime targets.

But we can remember that God and his angels are here with us. **"Elisha prayed, 'Open his eyes, Lord, so that he may see.' Then the Lord opened the servant's eyes, and he looked and saw the hills full of horses and chariots of fire all around Elisha"** (2 Kings 6:17).

All future citizens of heaven wear the full armor of God. The victorious King of kings rides ahead of us. He prays for us, and his angels protect us. Let's not fight against our own people.

Father, may we find the holy words for uplifting, wholesome talk to shut the mouths of those lurking around to poison perceptions. In the name of Jesus, we pray. Amen.

Forgiveness

Karen Maio

"In him we have redemption through his blood, the forgiveness of sins, in accordance with the riches of God's grace" (Ephesians 1:7).

What wonderful, comforting words of God's grace and ready forgiveness!

But did you ever feel a guilty twinge as you prayed, "Forgive us our sins as we forgive those who sin against us" in the Lord's Prayer? Sometimes it's not easy for us to forgive others.

Last summer I got a refresher course in forgiveness.

We had just returned home. My son stepped inside the house, and I yelled for him to come back out. I told him I was pretty sure I had locked the door, which was now standing wide open! We called the police, and our fears were confirmed: we had been burglarized. We were terrified, angry, and saddened. The burglars were eventually arrested, tried, and sentenced. One apologized, but I ignored him. Justice was served; it was a relief . . . but incomplete.

I thanked God that nobody in my family had been hurt or killed. God gradually restored peace in our home, but I knew I had to forgive the one who apologized—sincerely or not—according to God's will. Too scared to do it in person, I wrote a letter telling him that we all do wrong things but have forgiveness through faith in Jesus. I forgave him too. I pray that the Holy Spirit works faith in his heart.

Peace felt from forgiveness feels better than anger and fear and guilt. We're forgiven. That's why we're forgiving too.

The perfect life

Karen Spiegelberg

It was all over the national news. A massive hurricane had wiped out enormous parts of southern Florida. Newscasters were interviewing a woman whose home was in the path of the destruction. The woman was weeping heavily as she exclaimed, "We finally had everything, and now it's all gone. We had the perfect life."

I'm not judging this woman because I don't know exactly how I would have reacted in the same situation. I pray that I would be one of those folks who generally say, "It's just stuff that can be replaced. Thank God we're alright, though."

In 1 John 2:15, the apostle warns the early churches and us: **"Do not love the world or anything in the world. If anyone loves the world, love for the Father is not in them."** Believers are to love God and one another, not the world or possessions. In this verse, the word *world* is referring to our broken and self-centered way of living. In 1 John 2:16,17, John continues, **"For everything in the world—the lust of the flesh, the lust of the eyes, and the pride of life—comes not from the Father but from the world. The world and its desires pass away, but whoever does the will of God lives forever."**

This fallen world and our possessions will pass away, whether by hurricane, fire, or the end of time. But we have everything because of what Jesus has won for us— the possession of eternity in heaven. The perfect life!

Spirituality at work

Carolyn Webb

Do you take Jesus to work with you? Here are a few passages to help you incorporate Jesus into your work:

- Align your work with your values: **"Whatever you do, work at it with all your heart, as working for the Lord, not for human masters"** (Colossians 3:23).

- Lead by example: **"In everything set them an example by doing what is good. In your teaching show integrity, seriousness and soundness of speech that cannot be condemned, so that those who oppose you may be ashamed because they have nothing bad to say about us"** (Titus 2:7,8).

- Follow the Golden Rule: **"In everything, do to others what you would have them do to you, for this sums up the Law and the Prophets"** (Matthew 7:12).

- Practice gratitude: **"Rejoice always, pray continually, give thanks in all circumstances; for this is God's will for you in Christ Jesus"** (1 Thessalonians 5:16-18).

- Keep the peace: **"Be completely humble and gentle; be patient, bearing with one another in love. Make every effort to keep the unity of the Spirit through the bond of peace"** (Ephesians 4:2,3).

Spiritual growth and witnessing about Jesus don't happen exclusively in a church. We grow spiritually when we incorporate our values into every aspect of our lives. We bring others to Jesus the same way through our daily living.

Sad prayers

Julie Luetke

Recently, a mother told me her prayers didn't seem like enough and asked me to pray for her son. She had been praying a long time. Her son was dying spiritually from poor choices he had made. It was a very sad prayer.

The day I was asked to pray for this young man, I had just read Proverbs chapters 3-6. These chapters talk of a person led astray by his folly. Words like the ones below helped me pray for my friend's son.

"Trust in the Lord with all your heart and lean not on your own understanding" (Proverbs 3:5).

"The Lord disciplines those he loves, as a father the son he delights in" (Proverbs 3:12).

Many more proverbs helped me know what to pray. My prayers were still sad but not without substance and hope. God also gives us help to pray for the parents who are hurting.

"Come, let us return to the Lord. He has torn us to pieces but he will heal us; he has injured us but he will bind up our wounds" (Hosea 6:1).

The son will have consequences for his many foolish actions, but the Lord forgives and brings us back.

"You will seek me and find me when you seek me with all your heart" (Jeremiah 29:13).

"So great is his love for those who fear him; as far as the east is from the west, so far has he removed our transgressions from us" (Psalm 103:11,12).

God is surely listening to the prayers of the parents and friends of the foolish.

Stuck on a plateau

Christine Wentzel

Anyone on a long-range weight loss plan knows what it means to be stuck on a no-progress plateau. It's that interim of time when your body decides to take a hiatus, refusing to lower the number on a scale.

While in this time-out, it's good to ponder how our faith can stand on a similar plateau. We're too tired, too distracted, and maybe too bored—in general, allowing a dead-end life to slow down our new life in Christ.

Weight loss experts say plateaus happen because our bodies adapt quickly to routine. They suggest changing them from time to time and enlisting buddies to help us stay on track. How well this also applies to moving off a plateaued faith!

"So I say, live by the Spirit, and you will not gratify the desires of the sinful flesh" (Galatians 5:16).

The great news is that we decide how long we hang around on a plateau. The indwelling of the Holy Spirit delights in working nonstop to help us move forward. We can immediately mark our progress when we see the fruit of his labor through the virtues of love, joy, peace, patience, kindness, goodness, faithfulness, gentleness, and self-control. Yes!

Look at spiritual growth routines, note the room for improvement, and change things up. The amazing result from a healthy faith walk is the effect it has on every aspect of our lives. Our personal, divine trainer equips us to move through all kinds of no-progress plateaus—including the weight loss ones. C'mon, let's go!

God is almighty

Janet Gehlhar

I've found great comfort when I meditate on God's character . . . almighty, holy, merciful, faithful, sovereign . . . and realize that this is MY God and he uses all of his abilities in his plan for me. By knowing that God has never broken even one promise and knowing that he is omniscient (knows all), it is much easier for me to be at peace when traumatic events happen or just when every-day annoyances are getting the best of me.

I belong to God, and he's in control of my life. He is too wise to make a mistake. He alone can see what's best for me for today and for the future. What a relief that it isn't all up to me!

"Ah, Sovereign Lord, you have made the heavens and the earth by your great power and outstretched arm. Nothing is too hard for you" (Jeremiah 32:17).

I remind myself that when life seems too hard for me, it's God who's on my side, and I am secure.

We are SO blessed!

Christine Wentzel

When news is told about someone surviving a near catastrophe, comments like this one may follow: "Boy, someone was looking after you." Does this imply that when a person doesn't survive, he or she didn't have that same kind of preferential treatment?

"God does not show favoritism" (Romans 2:11).

Sometimes Christians are just as guilty of portraying a type of favoritism. We may use the word *blessed* for good things that we "deserved." But when that blessing is slow in coming or it never arrives the way we anticipate, the bragging gets awkward. Way deep down where we think the Son don't shine, we may feel disappointment or anger that his blessing didn't match our expectations.

Remember Jesus' life. So much of it looked like a person born under a bad star instead of a miraculous one. Jesus' conception appeared to happen from infidelity. He was an odd duck, a perfect kid. He was a confirmed bachelor in an age where marriage and family were a man's pride. He was homeless—a vagabond hanging around sinners. He hung on a cross, a convicted criminal. Was he blessed by God? Um, might take an act of faith to believe that. Thank the Lord it's a gift he freely gives!

It was God's desire to bless his only Son with the task of restoring the defiant people he pursues and loves. Jesus blessed us by obeying his Father's command to fulfill the law perfectly for us and end its judgment of death once and forever by walking out of the grave once and for all.

That's a Blessing with a capital *B*!

What are you worried about?

Erica Koester

I tend to worry . . . a lot. Ever since I was a kid, my family has pointed out the ridiculous nature of some of my worries. Needless to say, I am fully aware that this is one of my most repetitious shortcomings.

The sneaky thing about worry is that it often masquerades itself as being well-intentioned. "I worry about my kids because I care for them." "I worry about my health because I want to live a long life." However, at the root of our worries exists a lack of trust in the Lord.

I recently spent two full days worrying that I'd made the right decision. Finally, I prayed to God, put that situation in his hands, and immediately felt a weight lifted. Not because that earthly situation suddenly disappeared but because the peace of God—knowing he is in control— overcame my worries.

I should probably plaster the words of Philippians 4:6,7 onto every surface in my home: **"Do not be anxious about anything, but in every situation, by prayer and petition, with thanksgiving, present your requests to God. And the peace of God, which transcends all understanding, will guard your hearts and your minds in Christ Jesus."**

Our heavenly Father wants us to approach him with our worries and lay them at his feet. He is in control. He always has been, and he always will be! It's really beautiful that on the other side of worry, God offers a peace that quite literally transcends our human understanding. May you know that peace today and every day.

Brokenhearted

Carolyn Webb

Anxiety and depression affect millions of people in America each year. When I'm struggling with anxiety or depression, my mind whirls with many negative thoughts: "No one understands," "I am all alone," "I can't handle this." What I need at times like this is to stay connected to God's Word and his promises.

God understands:

"The LORD is close to the brokenhearted and saves those who are crushed in spirit" (Psalm 34:18).

I am not alone:

"Surely I am with you always, to the very end of the age" (Matthew 28:20).

My weakness shows God's strength:

"He said to me, 'My grace is sufficient for you, for my power is made perfect in weakness.' Therefore I will boast all the more gladly about my weaknesses, so that Christ's power may rest on me. That is why, for Christ's sake, I delight in weaknesses, in insults, in hardships, in persecutions, in difficulties. For when I am weak, then I am strong" (2 Corinthians 12:9-11).

Depression attacks the body, mind, and spirit. Treatment needs to address the total effect—physical, emotional, intellectual, and spiritual. If you or someone you love is feeling helpless and hopeless, seek help from your medical doctor and from the greatest physician of all—your heavenly Father.

"Hear my prayer, LORD; let my cry for help come to you. Do not hide your face from me when I am in distress. Turn your ear to me; when I call, answer me quickly" (Psalm 102:1,2).

God is faithful to his promises!

Lori Malnes

I was listening to music from the musical *The Child of the Promise* this morning and was struck how God answers prayers and fulfills his promises. He gave Elizabeth, the mother of John the Baptist, her child late in life after years and years of prayers and tears. He sent his promised Son into the world thousands of years after he initially promised him. And there are so many examples in the Old Testament of waiting on God. Yet not all his answers come after a long waiting time. Peter called for help, and Jesus immediately pulled him out of the waves. A woman touched Jesus' garment, and immediately her prayer was answered and she was healed. Whether it's an immediate answer, a long wait, somewhere in between, or even a no answer, we know that God ALWAYS hears and answers our prayers. He is faithful—ALWAYS.

When we celebrate the birth of the long-awaited Messiah, let us be reminded of his faithfulness. Let us persist in our prayers for our friends and family who have turned away from their Messiah or who still need him in their lives. Let us trust him who is faithful and who hears our every prayer. May the baby Jesus impact the hearts and lives of all those on our hearts and minds at Christmas. May our thoughts, words, and actions reflect his life in us to others always.

"Today in the town of David a Savior has been born to you; he is the Messiah, the Lord" (Luke 2:11).

Unwelcome gifts

Tracy Hankwitz

Another snowfall—this one not welcome. It's April. Yesterday the air was warm; today, there's white falling from above. I know there's a reason for this delay of season change. Spring will come in God's timing, not mine. So I sigh, murmur thanks, and get out the shovel.

There's been a lot of unwanted snowfalls lately, unwelcome gifts. A dear friend loses her battle with cancer; another struggles with depression—wandering in what seems like life's desert—trying desperately to find direction. Snow may fall quietly, but at times it's a blizzard.

We've all tasted disappointment when life doesn't go the way we wish it would. We look at what has been placed in our hands and say, "What is this?" Like Israelites in the desert, we look at this manna, white falling from above, and ask, "What is this? What is this that God wants me to walk through? This is grace? This is what God thinks is best for me?"

Though we don't understand, he asks us to trust him. He asks us to gather up this manna every morning, this thing that doesn't make sense, and receive it as a gift—as grace. Instead of asking *why*, we are to be grateful and turn our pleas into praise. It isn't easy, but we can trust our heavenly Father with everything. He knows what's best for us, and this manna is meant to nourish. As we hold this manna in our hands, he holds us in his.

"Trust in the LORD with all your heart and lean not on your own understanding" (Proverbs 3:5).

Blessed is she who has believed that the Lord would fulfill his promises to her!

Luke 1:45

*Make a list of at least five promises
God makes to you in his Word.*

_____

_____

_____

_____

_____

_____

_____

_____

_____

_____

God's great love

Erica Koester

A few months after having my son, I began to struggle internally. I was navigating motherhood for the first time and trying to juggle many other obligations. Foreign, negative thoughts started to creep in. It reached a point so low that I genuinely believed I was failing as a wife, as a mother, as a friend, and as an employee. It was at that time that I sought Christian counseling. In talking with a professional, we slowly unearthed the very root of the problem: I had consistently believed the lies of the enemy.

That's a heavy story to share, but the work of the devil needs to be exposed. Dear sisters, what lies have you believed about yourself that directly contradict what God says about you in his Word? We are fearfully and wonderfully made; God carefully formed us together in our mothers' wombs.

Not only did God create us, but he loves us dearly. Paul shares beautiful words about Christ's love in Ephesians 3:17-19: **"And I pray that you, being rooted and established in love, may have power, together with all the Lord's holy people, to grasp how wide and long and high and deep is the love of Christ, and to know this love that surpasses knowledge—that you may be filled to the measure of all the fullness of God."**

The love of God is so great that it surpasses our human knowledge. Maybe that's why we have such a hard time grasping it! May you be reminded today that your Father in heaven created you and loves you more than you even know.

Cherished opportunities

Lori Malnes

I remember a cherished time with my eldest daughter—the few months that she was home between her December college graduation and her July wedding. What a blessing! When they were young, our daughters' bedrooms were upstairs with our bedroom; and since I am a light sleeper, I usually got up and tucked them back into bed when either of them got up in the middle of the night for a drink of water or whatever. When my daughter was back home, I particularly cherished tucking her into bed just like when she was little because the opportunities to do that were dwindling. As we walked back to her room, she'd often put her head on my shoulder. Then after I tucked her in, she'd sleepily tell me she loves me—precious times!

I have only a short time here on earth. My time here is precious. How many opportunities to share my faith, to share Jesus, do I miss because I'd rather "stay in my warm, comfortable bed"? But as with my daughters, look what I'd be missing! Sure, there are times when I tucked in a grumpy daughter, but what about those other times? The same is true with sharing my faith—not every time will bring the warm fuzzies—but I can't waste the opportunities because life is too short. I don't know when my life or the lives of others will end here on earth. I can't, and dare not, waste the opportunities that God gives me to share him with others.

"You know very well that the day of the Lord will come like a thief in the night" (1 Thessalonians 5:2).

Satan is the king of Post-its

Talia Steinhauer

Recently, my second-grade class studied a Bible lesson called "Jesus Is Tempted." One of my boys raised his hand and said, "When the devil tempts us, it's like he's putting a Post-it note on our brains."

I laughed to myself for a second, as I do many times during the day, but then thought about it and realized he was spot on!

"Away from me, Satan! For it is written: 'Worship the Lord your God, and serve him only'" (Matthew 4:10).

The devil tried insanely hard to tempt Jesus. He targeted all of the areas that he knew he had a chance to make Jesus mess up in. Jesus was hungry and isolated, and yet he never once faltered.

So what do Post-its have to do with Satan? Every time the devil tempts you with something, it's like he sticks a Post-it on your brain. A few minutes later, another Post-it is added. All of a sudden, your brain is covered in Post-its and you're knee-deep in the devil's temptations. How can you possibly think clearly or follow God's plan for your life when you're so distracted with Post-its?

So how do we get rid of these Post-its? We pray to God for strength every time we're tempted. We pray that he helps us keep our eyes on him. What happens when we do that? The Post-its are removed from our brains one at a time.

The best part about Post-its? They're temporary. They can be removed. So, nice try devil, but you can't take over our brains with temptations, because we have the best Post-it remover ever.

This may hurt a little

Tracy Hankwitz

I love to prune. An overgrown tangle of branches is a challenge I welcome. First, I remove dead branches. Next, I remove the crossing ones. Finally, my favorite part, I make cuts that will reveal the true beauty of the shrub and promote better flowering and fruiting.

A few days ago, I found myself in the middle of an overgrown planting of viburnum, and the similarities struck me. At times my ego gets overgrown and needs pruning. I rely on myself rather than on God to handle my day-to-day crises. The crossing branches in my life are my own selfish wants that cross God's will. Then there's daily struggle to balance priorities and stay connected to the vine. I must look like a mess to his eye of perfection.

Thankfully God is patient with me. He lovingly prunes me, cutting away everything overgrown and ugly. He knows exactly which cuts to make to train me to turn back to him, removing my dead sinful branches with complete forgiveness. When I stubbornly insist on crossing him to do what I want, he makes cuts that guide me to grow in line with his will. Sometime his cuts hurt a little. Sometimes they hurt a lot. But his ultimate goal is to prune me to reveal a beautiful life that glorifies him with an abundance of fruits of faith.

"I am the true vine, and my Father is the gardener. He cuts off every branch in me that bears no fruit, while every branch that does bear fruit he prunes so that it will be even more fruitful" (John 15:1,2).

At the manger

Karen Spiegelberg

It's that time of year when we enjoy the lights and Christmas decorations neighbors have displayed in their yards. I particularly love any outdoor nativity scene. My deep appreciation for nativity scenes goes back to when I was a child. We lived just blocks from our church, and it was an annual tradition for my dad to walk our family to see the rustic stable with Joseph, Mary, and baby Jesus. I remember staring in at that tiny "baby" and wondering what it would have been like to be one of the shepherds on that most holy night.

Oh, how I would have loved to have been there when the angels announced the birth of the Messiah, the One who was promised to come! However, my time on this earth was not meant to begin until the late 1950s. But why should my mission be any different than the shepherds of long ago? I should also feel as in Luke 2:17 where we read: **"When they had seen him, they spread the word concerning what had been told them about this child."** Amen and hallelujah!

In these last days before Christmas, my prayer for you is that you take time to peer closely at that baby and then "spread the word" with family, friends, coworkers, and anyone at your holiday gatherings or events. Isaiah's prophecy is fulfilled! The Prince of peace was born for you and for me and for all people!

The power of meditation

Carolyn Webb

The term *meditation* refers to a broad variety of practices designed to promote relaxation, build internal energy, and develop compassion. Meditation can improve physical health, emotional balance, mental clarity, and relationships.

The Bible promotes meditation too. There are multiple references in the book of Psalms reminding us to meditate on God's Word.

- **"Blessed is the one who does not walk in step with the wicked or stand in the way that sinners take or sit in the company of mockers, but whose delight is in the law of the Lᴏʀᴅ, and who meditates on his law day and night"** (Psalm 1:1,2).

- **"I will consider all your works and meditate on all your mighty deeds"** (Psalm 77:12).

- **"I meditate on your precepts and consider your ways. I delight in your decrees; I will not neglect your word"** (Psalm 119:15,16).

- **"Oh, how I love your law! I meditate on it all day long. I have more insight than all my teachers, for I meditate on your statutes"** (Psalm 119:97,99).

Meditating on God's Word can bring true peace and wisdom. When the troubles of this world come crashing in, turn to God's Word and meditate on his promises. **"I have told you these things, so that in me you may have peace. In this world you will have trouble. But take heart! I have overcome the world"** (John 16:33).

What are you afraid of?

Julie Luetke

Afraid you aren't good enough? Afraid of test results? Afraid of bad news? Afraid your relationship is falling apart? Afraid of what's happening in our economy? Afraid you'll get sick? Afraid you're failing as a mother? Afraid of death?

We all have fears. Our fears change as the situations in our lives change. No matter what brings us fear, God has sweet words of comfort.

"Do not fear, for I have redeemed you; I have summoned you by name; you are mine. When you pass through the waters, I will be with you; and when you pass through the rivers, they will not sweep over you. When you walk through the fire, you will not be burned; the flames will not set you ablaze. For I am the Lord your God, the Holy One of Israel, your Savior" (Isaiah 43:1-3).

No matter your current fear, your heavenly Father tells you to fear not because he has redeemed you. Now, God doesn't say you won't have fearful things happen to you, but when they do come, God assures you:

"For I am the Lord your God who takes hold of your right hand and says to you, Do not fear; I will help you" (Isaiah 41:13).

As a small child is able to walk into a scary doctor's office as long as Daddy's hand is holding his, you can face every fearful situation because your heavenly Father takes you by the hand and gently whispers, "Do not fear; I will help you."

Do you need a doctor?

Carolyn Webb

As my husband struggled with an autoimmune disease, a nurse said to him, "I'll bet you're tired of living in a bubble." To which he replied, "No. What I'm tired of is everyone telling me how sick I am." Spiritually, you might experience something similar. Do you get tired of hearing how sin-sick you are? Are you tempted to think that because you're a "good person" you're not sinful?

The Pharisees of Jesus' time thought if they avoided people like tax collectors and piously followed their religion, they could avoid being infected by sin. Jesus had a different message for them: **"It is not the healthy who need a doctor, but the sick. But go and learn what this means: 'I desire mercy, not sacrifice.' For I have not come to call the righteous, but sinners"** (Matthew 9:12,13).

If you and I don't recognize our illness, we don't seek out the help of a physician. If we don't recognize our sin, we see no need for a Savior. Don't tire of hearing the law of God. It's only when we recognize the sin in our lives that we accept the help that Jesus provides. **"In him we have redemption through his blood, the forgiveness of sins, in accordance with the riches of God's grace"** (Ephesians 1:7).

Leaning on a spider's web

Diana Kerr

Tell me about your biggest stressors, the things you strive for and the things you're attached to, and I bet I can tell you what it is that you trust in this life. Many of us are unconsciously led by these misguided reliances and beliefs.

Some of us lean on our marriages or our families, believing that the key to a good life is a strong family unit. Some of us lean on money, believing that financial stability will pave the way to peace. Some of us lean on our accomplishments, believing that we're worth more when we cross off a bunch of stuff on our to-do lists.

We all do this in some form or another. Our sinful hearts are not as allegiant to God as we think they are and as we want them to be. So we lean on earthly things, often good blessings from our Lord, but those things are so much less reliable than we realize.

The book of Job talks about this challenge and describes the actions of those who have forgotten God: **"What they trust in is fragile; what they rely on is a spider's web. They lean on the web, but it gives way; they cling to it, but it does not hold"** (8:14,15).

Friend, what are you clinging to that's as weak as a spider's web? What if you put that thing back in its rightful place in your heart and lean on God? I promise you it'd be a game changer.

Symptoms

April Cooper

Runny nose. Sneezing. Watery eyes. It's usually easy to identify the symptoms of the common cold. Throw in fever, chills, and muscle aches, and it may be categorized as the flu. See any red bumps that progress to blisters? Could be the telltale signs of chicken pox, right? Our physical bodies alert us with symptoms that typically lead to a diagnosis with medication and proper care instructions. But what about within our spiritual lives? Are there "symptoms" that can be addressed there as well? Indeed!

As a believer in Christ, be encouraged! Here are just a few Scripture verses to apply to symptoms that may develop from time to time:

Feeling alone?

"Be strong and courageous. Do not be afraid or terrified because of them, for the Lord your God goes with you; he will never leave you nor forsake you" (Deuteronomy 31:6).

Feeling like you want to give up?

"Do not fear, for I am with you; do not be dismayed, for I am your God. I will strengthen you and help you; I will uphold you with my righteous right hand" (Isaiah 41:10).

Feeling worried?

"Humble yourselves, therefore, under God's mighty hand, that he may lift you up in due time. Cast all your anxiety on him because he cares for you" (1 Peter 5:6,7).

The Bible addresses everything we face in life. Be sure to give God the praise, the glory, and the honor through it all. He is, indeed, the cure.

Breaking branches

Christine Wentzel

There's a scene in the movie *National Lampoon's Christmas Vacation* where Aunt Bethany's cat is gnawing on a string of lights. The cat ends up as a blackened outline forever burned into the Griswold's carpet. It brings to mind our tendencies to play with the "pretty" things that could eternally burn us.

Let's look at our pet sins. Really look at the ones so familiar to us that we're going blind to the fact that we're chomping away at the branch that gives us true life. We need to pause for a moment to see how close we are to the devil yelling, "Timberrrrr!"

"I am the vine; you are the branches. If you remain in me and I in you, you will bear much fruit; apart from me you can do nothing" (John 15:5).

No pet sins are too strong to be broken. We feel the strength of their claws dig into us like phantom pain. But their real hold was clamped on to the Lamb of God at the cross. As a result, with our daily repentance, we have the Holy Spirit's renewal and our Christian community for cultivating God-pleasing lives.

Dear Jesus, thank you for grafting me into your life-giving vine. Forgive me for growing numb toward the sins I keep. Open my eyes to their true harm. Help shift my desire into actions that bear good fruit in your name. Amen.

Listen to me

Christine Wentzel

Chatty strangers are put on this earth to test impatient-bent Christians. Whether they catch us on a good or bad day, there seems to be an underlying urge to avoid them, or be annoyed by them.

What makes a stranger open up to another stranger? We all desire a sense of connection. We all know what it's like to feel lonely or tuned out in rudeness, anger, or indifference. But, in this age of everyone standing on his or her personal soapboxes, it's so much easier to speak than to listen!

"Remember this, my dear brothers and sisters: Everyone should be quick to listen, slow to speak, and should not get angry easily" (James 1:19 GW).

Note that the apostle James mentions "everyone" in his reminder. That means we all can be quick to listen if we prayerfully work at it. And listening isn't only hearing, but it's "listening" to body language as well. We know the physical cues of people in need. Let's slow down and listen. Let's acknowledge their presence with Jesus' presence in us—giving them our full attention and some precious time.

Doesn't even a small moment of real human connection ring true for both parties and bring God glory?

Drop that stone!

Karen Spiegelberg

As a kid, I enjoyed collecting pretty stones from a nearby riverbed. I long ago gave up my collection, and yet a pile still mysteriously surrounds me. Maybe you have one too. You know, that pile of stones we cast in judgment of others' actions. Usually public or "yuck" sins—sins that are hard to process like sexual assault or child pornography. Our first response is typically, "I would never do something like that!" Our next response is to pick up a proverbial stone and throw it in sure judgment.

Stop! Drop that stone! Instead, take a journey with me to the temple courts during Jesus' time. Jesus was in the temple courts with many people gathered around. The teachers of the law and the Pharisees brought in an adulteress. They wanted permission from Jesus to stone her, but Jesus calmly replied, **"Let any one of you who is without sin be the first to throw a stone at her"** (John 8:7). Upon hearing this, the people started to go away. They knew that they were no better than the adulteress, that they too were sinful.

I so appreciate God's Word reminding me that no matter how small I may think my daily sin is, I'm just as guilty as anyone in the news or the adulteress of Jesus' day. **"The sting of death is sin, and the power of sin is the law. But thanks be to God! He gives us the victory through our Lord Jesus Christ"** (1 Corinthians 15:56,57).

The pain of mortality

Christine Wentzel

Nothing tests our faith quite the way the pain of our mortality does. In other words, the way our bodies' physical breakdowns hold a mirror of reality up to our faith and say, "Show me how strong you really are."

If our first encounter with our mortality shakes up what we thought to be true about the strength of our faith, God will get down in the dirt with us and wrestle until we realize we're not getting more tired and weak. Miraculously, we grow stronger!

"Not only so, but we also glory in our sufferings, because we know that suffering produces perseverance; perseverance, character; and character, hope" (Romans 5:3,4).

In searching the Scriptures, we find Miriam's bout with leprosy, Naomi's loss of her husband and sons, the woman who bled for 12 long years, and Mary Magdalene's possession by seven demon spirits. These women wrestled and grew stronger in faith. Their stories of God's providence were preserved for the rest of us to draw comfort. Now our stories of hope are there to share with others who are wrestling with their assaulted faith.

There's no shame in the humbling of our mortal bodies. It reminds us heaven is our home. Jesus suffered the pain of mortality first. He sweated blood in the Garden of Gethsemane when confronted with the knowledge of the pain to come in bearing the sins of the world to his death. He tussled with his Father until he was strengthened by the joy of our eternal reward. He obeyed, **"Yet not my will, but yours be done"** (Luke 22:42).

Fall clothes

Karen Maio

It's that time of year again. There's a nip in the early morning air, the sky is darker earlier in the evening, and we must start making the transition from summer clothes to fall clothes.

For me, that means the painful exercise of going through the closets and bins, having my son try on clothes to see what fits, weeding out items that never get worn, and then shopping for the rest.

There are items I maybe haven't worn as often as I should. Not actual clothes, but rather attributes often referred to as "fruits of the Spirit."

"Clothe yourselves with compassion, kindness, humility, gentleness and patience. Bear with each other and forgive one another if any of you has a grievance against someone. Forgive as the Lord forgave you" (Colossians 3:12,13).

Have I been kind and compassionate, or has "hurrying disease" made me short and impatient? Have I gently served with humbleness or grumbled over being asked to help out . . . again? Do I have a forgiving heart, or am I holding a grudge?

Yuck . . . those "clothes" need to be washed! Thankfully, Jesus has just the right detergent—he washed them in his holy blood, and they came out looking whiter than snow. **"They have washed their robes and made them white in the blood of the Lamb"** (Revelation 7:14).

As I transition to fall clothes, with the Holy Spirit's help, I resolve to clothe myself with compassion, kindness, humility, gentleness, and patience and encourage my child to do the same.

Forgiveness that never ends

Diana Kerr

Have you ever worked really hard to forgive someone only to have him or her disappoint you again? I definitely have. Let's be honest: as sinners who carry pride and bitterness, sometimes it takes us years to get over stuff and soften our hearts toward someone.

And then that person we worked so hard to forgive does something that requires us to forgive all over again. I have fallen naively into the trap of thinking that if I forgive someone once, it will be smooth sailing from there on out. However, our flawed, imperfect world doesn't always work that way.

The Jewish leaders of Jesus' time said you should only forgive someone three times. Jesus (our sinless Savior who has forgiven each of our sins an embarrassing amount of times), shattered that rule.

"Then Peter came to Jesus and asked, 'Lord, how many times shall I forgive my brother or sister who sins against me? Up to seven times?' Jesus answered, 'I tell you, not seven times, but seventy-seven times'" (Matthew 18:21,22).

In other words, our Lord wants us to forgive endlessly, over and over and over again. If by grace we are forgiven countless times, then that grace compels us to pass on that limitless forgiveness. Note that forgiveness doesn't mean you can't set boundaries or that you are condoning an action, but it does say, "I forgive you now, completely and unconditionally, and I will forgive you over and over again."

Every single day

Janet Gehlhar

Every day I start out thinking that today will be different. I'll get my list done; I'll show love and kindness; I'll be the person God wants me to be . . . and you guessed it—I fail. Those good intentions aren't enough. I feel burdened with guilt. But then I read this Bible passage:

"Praise be to the Lord, to God our Savior, who daily bears our burdens" (Psalm 68:19).

Daily . . . not weekly or monthly but daily. How comforting to know that God daily forgives me, daily gives me what I need, watches over me, understands all the big stresses and the "little" things bothering me, and assures me he is in charge and will handle it all. It isn't up to me.

I'm starting today with praise to God and thanks to him for being in charge of my day. I can have peace in my heart knowing God is carrying my burdens and working all things for my eternal good.

Give thanks in all things?

Julie Luetke

I wasn't thankful when I sprained my ankle. I'm not thankful for my friend's pain. I'm not thankful a loved one does not love God. No doubt, you have a similar list. How do we obey God and be thankful in all circumstances when some circumstances are just plain awful? God gives us tips in this verse to help: **"Rejoice always, pray continually, give thanks in all circumstances; for this is God's will for you in Christ Jesus"** (1 Thessalonians 5:16-18).

This verse begins, "Rejoice always." If you think about all that God has done for you and me, it's easy to be joyful and thankful even when some things aren't going so well. Look around at the blessings in your life. I'm thankful for a warm house and hot running water. We have a Savior who paid the price for our sin and is preparing a home for us in heaven. That makes me joyful. How about you?

God gives us another tip for thankfulness in all circumstances. God tells us to "pray continually." Many of the circumstances in our lives we would rather not face are the very things God knows we need. It's through weakness that we realize we have an all-powerful God. When I know my God is strong enough to help me in any trouble, I'm comforted and thankful.

As you go about your day, think of things to thank God for. You will find your heart is quickly filled with joy and thanksgiving . . . for this is God's will for you in Christ Jesus.

For the Spirit God gave us does not make us timid, but gives us power, love and self-discipline.

2 Timothy 1:7

Are there things you know you should do but don't because you're afraid, worried, or timid? List them here.

_____

_____

_____

_____

_____

_____

_____

_____

A letter to a lost loved one

Carolyn Webb

Dearest,

I have prayed for you and cried for you. I have even questioned God's promises. There appears to be a contradiction between his promise in John 10:28 (**"I give them eternal life, and they shall never perish; no one will snatch them out of my hand"**) and the parable of the seed that falls among rocks and weeds. Are you a seed that fell on rocky ground: **"The ones who receive the word with joy when they hear it, but have no root. They believe for a while, but in the time of testing they fall away"** (Luke 8:13)? Or are you a seed that has fallen among the weeds, hearing God's Word but as you went on your way were **"choked by life's worries, riches and pleasures, and . . . do not mature"** (Luke 8: 14)?

With God there is no contradiction. Maybe he will take that rock and break it down or till the weeds into the soil to create a more fertile soil. Maybe when the seed is sown again, it will take root.

While I am saddened that it appears you have separated from God, I will remember that **"people look at the outward appearance, but the Lord looks at the heart"** (1 Samuel 16:7). I will not nag you, but I will continue to pray for you, **"being confident of this, that he who began a good work in you will carry it on to completion until the day of Christ Jesus"** (Philippians 1:6). In that final day, I pray that you will be with your Savior in paradise.

All my love.

Tug-of-war

Julie Luetke

Picture a game of tug-of-war. If your team is strong, it's easier to win. When I'm with strong Christians, it's easy to be confident of the things God has done for me. I'm part of a strong team.

The other team represents sickness, doubts, guilt, temptations, and all things that pull me away from God. The other team is strong and wants to drag me to hell.

As our bodies need good food to be strong, our faith needs the food of God's Word. Attending church and hearing God's Word with our team members makes our faith grow stronger. We gain in strength individually with personal Bible reading, thus strengthening the team.

"Let us consider how we may spur one another on toward love and good deeds, not giving up meeting together, as some are in the habit of doing, but encouraging one another" (Hebrews 10:24,25).

Now think of your tug-of-war battle. The opposing team pulls hard, causing a few of your team members to stumble. One member stumbles with a divorce, and another's child is arrested. Guilt and sadness cause weakness in their grip of the rope. The strength of your team members holding on to God's Word helps to pick up the stumbled members.

As you feed the fallen God's Word, he or she gains a stronger grip. Through struggles the whole team marvels at what God has done.

You **"may have power, together with all the Lord's holy people, to grasp how wide and long and high and deep is the love of Christ"** (Ephesians 3:18,19).

Choose your mood

Janet Gehlhar

What I think about determines my mood for the day. I noticed this when I thought about all the problems in the world or wallowed in self-pity over some injustice. I felt negative, and my thoughts continued on that path for the day. Then I was challenged to have an attitude of gratitude. I was skeptical. But I gave it a try.

I continued to give all of my problems and concerns over to God in prayer, but then I ended my prayers by giving thanks for a list of things. At first I felt awkward because thankfulness didn't automatically flow. But, within a very short time, I found myself finding things to be thankful for all day long . . . a hot shower, electricity, comfy shoes, a pretty flower, enough food for one more meal so I didn't have to race to the grocery store. What amazed me most was that while nothing had changed around me or in my personal circumstances, I felt more upbeat and positive. I admit I didn't think it would last, but it has. In fact, my mind is training to pick out the good and to be thankful instead of being critical.

"Finally, brothers and sisters, whatever is true, whatever is noble, whatever is right, whatever is pure, whatever is lovely, whatever is admirable—if anything is excellent or praiseworthy—think about such things" (Philippians 4:8).

I copied that passage and have it taped to the window near where I do my dishes. It's a daily reminder to channel my thoughts to the excellent and praiseworthy.

Stumbling blocks

Christine Wentzel

"Therefore let us stop passing judgment on one another. Instead, make up your mind not to put any stumbling block or obstacle in the way of a brother or sister" (Romans 14:13).

Let's face it. We *will* hurt each other. Intentionally or not, we still war with our broken selves. We tend to go to our default position of original sin and judge with our eyes instead of what God sees.

It's never been more in your face than on social media. Just a casual scroll down the newsfeed brings all kinds of stumbling blocks to our faith walks. Christians can be the worst offenders, and yet we know better.

In the Garden of Gethsemane, Jesus' blood splattered down from his brow as he prayed about our weakness in temptation. Will our posts feed something ugly in us at the expense of another? Will they cheapen the grace God gave to sinners like us?

Every day is a new start with Christ. Let's watch and pray about this particular weakness. Don't give up praying if the same temptation keeps popping up or when new ones relentlessly appear. Let's ask the Lord to help make the path clear before we injure any more people.

Dear Father in heaven, I ask you to forgive my sins of _____. I ask you to remove these stumbling blocks once and for all. Reveal the times when I try to justify a decision to share an unloving post. Help me choose posts that quiet the cacophony of hateful social messages. I ask this in Jesus' name. Amen.

Hope for wanderers

Lori Malnes

One afternoon during a winter ocean/beach vacation, I took our dog, Trubble, for a walk on the deserted beach. Trubble chased waves, running up the dunes and back to check in. After a bit, he caught some scent and followed it. When I noticed his preoccupation, I called to him; but with the wind in my face and the roar of the waves, he couldn't hear me. Trubble went farther ahead, lost in whatever he smelled. Soon he was just a speck way down the beach. I wondered if I had lost our dog for good. I prayed for God to somehow bring us back together. Suddenly, I saw Trubble making a beeline back to me as fast as his legs could carry him.

As I walked back down the beach with Trubble leashed, I thought how neat it would be to be "leashed" to God so that I could never wander far away. If God could have heart attacks, I'm sure I've given him quite a few with my wanderings—the "scents" of this world distract me often.

Thankfully, you and I have a God who never gives up on us. And we need to keep praying, trusting God, and trusting in his promises as we consider the wanderers in our lives. May these wanderers turn their hearts toward their Master and make a beeline back to him. May we all hold on to the hope found only in our very big God.

"Are not five sparrows sold for two pennies? Yet not one of them is forgotten by God" (Luke 12:6).

Walk with the wise

Diana Kerr

You've probably heard the saying that goes something like this: "You are the sum total of the five people you spend the most time with." It's basically a modern version of Proverbs 13:20: **"Walk with the wise and become wise, for a companion of fools suffers harm."**

You will become like the people you hang out with, for better or worse. Yeah, you can blame your friends for your screwups, but maybe you need to blame yourself for hanging around those friends in the first place.

Remember when you were a kid and your parents had strong opinions about the friends who were "bad news"? Well, now you're an adult—you get to choose your friends on your own, no parental opinions involved. Just remember that there are consequences to those choices. Do you want friends who will cause you to compromise your values or friends who will strengthen your values? Do you want friends who will make you timid about bringing faith into a conversation or friends who challenge your faith and its presence in your life? Do you want friends who will make it easy for you to stray from God or friends who won't allow you to stray?

Don't be shy in asking God for help in surrounding yourself with friends who will make you wise in his ways. And a little hint about the five people you spend the majority of your time with—make Jesus one of those five people.

No rolling stops

Karen Spiegelberg

Since I became an elected official for the city in which I reside, I'm even more careful with my driving habits. After all, it would be pretty embarrassing if my name ended up in the newspaper, wouldn't it? I follow the speed limit, and I even come to a complete stop at each stop sign. No rolling stops.

As I was stopping consistently at each sign on my way to church recently, it occurred to me that our weekly church worship is sometimes like a rolling stop. Don't we often go through the motions of mindlessly reciting everything and then half-heartedly listening to the sermon? We kind of roll through the service without intentionally stopping to be present in the beautiful gift of congregational worship, be in the Word, and praise our Lord and Savior, Jesus Christ.

In Isaiah 29:13, the Lord says, **"These people come near to me with their mouth and honor me with their lips, but their hearts are far from me."** Yikes. Those words don't just apply to God's disappointment of the Israelites of Isaiah's day; they apply to us too!

We're blessed in the U.S. to have the constitutional freedom to worship publicly. That's a privilege that our early elected officials bestowed on us. I don't ever want to take that for granted, and I ask God to help me be 100 percent present in my weekly worship. No rolling stops. Let me wholeheartedly proclaim as David did in Psalm 122:1: **"I rejoiced with those who said to me, 'Let us go to the house of the Lord.'"**

Sifting through life

April Cooper

When preparing to bake with flour as an ingredient, it's important to sift the flour before adding it to the other ingredients. First, sifting ensures that only the best and most refined flour goes into the bowl with no clumps included. It lessens the likelihood that impurities such as debris or bugs found in the flour bag are added to your recipe. Sifting flour can also lead to a more evenly measured amount, which means you're not adding too much or too little based on the serving size of your recipe. Overall, sifting can produce a better baked product.

Scripture teaches us: **"While evildoers and impostors will go from bad to worse, deceiving and being deceived. But as for you, continue in what you have learned and have become convinced of, because you know those from whom you learned it, and how from infancy you have known the Holy Scriptures, which are able to make you wise for salvation through faith in Christ Jesus. All Scripture is God-breathed and is useful for teaching, rebuking, correcting and training in righteousness, so that the servant of God may be thoroughly equipped for every good work"** (2 Timothy 3:13-17).

As followers of Christ, the Holy Spirit helps us sift out everything according to the Word of God. All that we see, hear, say, and do needs to be aligned to Scripture when determining our actions/reactions. This ensures only the refined and righteous parts are incorporated into our personal journeys.

Penetrated hearts

Christine Wentzel

In the current climes of religious freedoms versus people's rights, there are a lot of hateful remarks made specifically toward Christians who try to live their lives by the social tenets of their faith. But when another religion makes a conservative stand, they are safe from social judgment. Why the double standard?

"The word of God is alive and active. Sharper than any double-edged sword, it penetrates even to dividing soul and spirit, joints and marrow; it judges the thoughts and attitudes of the heart" (Hebrews 4:12).

The root of hate speech isn't in the battle between differing ideologies. It's because of the internal conflict caused by the innate knowledge of God's law.

God's Word is alive and active! It's not just ink on paper. Its power stirs people's hearts for good or ill. That's what we witness in the passionate response to it: either hateful or loving. We should not be surprised but rather cheer on the Holy Spirit in his miraculous power!

When we hear or read the negative responses to a God-authored truth, talk to the Holy Spirit about the person who is spewing them. Let the Holy Spirit know you're awake to the fact that the Shepherd is calling his sheep to come home. Pray those sheep will listen.

Letting go of bitterness

Erica Koester

I recently made the alarming discovery that I was harboring bitterness in my heart over words someone spoke to me over two years ago. I took my sister's sound advice to pray for that person. Over time, I began to consider the grudge I was holding on to in the context of the fact that Jesus was willingly nailed to a cross to forgive the sins of the entire world. Suddenly, that grudge became extremely small.

I encourage you to open your Bible to the parable of the unmerciful servant (Matthew 18:21-35). Jesus delivered this parable after his disciple Peter asked Jesus to provide an exact number of times we should forgive someone. In this parable, the servant had a huge debt cancelled by his master but then turned around and demanded payment on a much smaller debt owed to him.

I find myself relating to that unmerciful servant all too well. God has removed the enormous debt of my countless wrongdoings, and in response . . . I harbored bitterness for over two years over one single slight. I also find myself relating to Peter! I am often tempted to keep track of the number of times my friends or spouse wrong me.

God's forgiveness knows no boundaries or limits, it never runs out, and it lasts forever. He extends it lovingly to everyone, and he calls us to do the same. My prayer for all of us is that our hearts would be so filled with thankfulness for what Jesus has done for us that we can't help but extend that same love and mercy to everyone we meet.

Why do we exist?

Carolyn Webb

One of the most fundamental human needs is to have a purpose in life. Holocaust survivor Viktor Frankl put it this way: "Life is not primarily a quest for pleasure, as Freud believed, or a quest for power, as Alfred Adler taught, but a quest for meaning. The greatest task for any person is to find meaning in his or her life." Where do you find meaning in your life?

I think it's sad when people reject the Bible's explanation to earth's creation and our place in it: **"In the beginning God created the heavens and the earth"** (Genesis 1:1). God created our world and the universe. God didn't just create a gooey cosmic soup from which everything emerged. He created bodies of water, land, plants, fish, birds, animals, and—as the crown jewel of his creation—**"God created mankind in his own image, in the image of God he created them; male and female he created them"** (Genesis 1:27). Unlike the other parts of creation, mankind was given a specific purpose: **"The Lord God took the man and put him in the Garden of Eden to work it and take care of it"** (Genesis 2:15).

Those who reject the Bible's explanation for our existence will continue to search in vain for the reason we exist. But we know that we have a God who loves us and who created us for a purpose. No further explanation is needed. We live to love and serve the God who created us to live in his universe.

Santa Claus

Karen Maio

Tradition says the real Santa Claus was Saint Nicholas, a fourth-century bishop in Turkey. Famous for acts of kindness, especially toward children, he became popular in Holland, where he was known as Sinterklaas. Eventually, Americans turned the name into Santa Claus.

For those with children, the time may come when you decide to go visit Santa. You can find him at any mall around! Plan ahead! If you want a smiling child for that photo, don't visit at nap time. Bring a mess-free snack to enjoy while waiting in line and an extra outfit in case baby decides to not be mess-free. If you have a toy that makes your child smile—bring it! He/she may decide to freak out when handed over to the fat, bearded stranger. Enjoy! Merry Christmas!

Ah, yes, Santa Claus—to "believe" or not to believe has been debated for years. Some are strictly against this secular icon; others are all for it. For me, there's nothing wrong with having some Santa fun if well-balanced with celebrating Jesus' birth, the true reason for the season. My son enjoyed opening presents and running to his stocking on Christmas morning to see what Santa brought him. He shows no need for therapy for the years of "deceit." However, he also attended Christmas worship services and was in a Christian Christmas program each year, memorizing Bible passages and hymns. It's all about where you want to place your true focus. **"For where your treasure is, there your heart will be also"** (Matthew 6:21).

Santa will eventually be outgrown, but Jesus is forever!

Pruning is a good thing

Julie Luetke

The berry patch gave us plenty of berries this year. So why do the bushes need pruning? Pruning is radical. When I pruned the berry bushes, I used a sharp tool that exposed the tender insides of the stalks. It's hard to imagine it was for their good.

Jesus tells us in John 15:2 that **"every branch that does bear fruit he prunes so that it will be even more fruitful."**

Pruning hurts. Suppose something terrible happens to you. The tender inside of your heart is raw with pain. Your life will never be the same. You keep asking, "Why, God? Why did you let this happen to me? Do you love me?"

I love my raspberries. The more they bear, the more I'll have to share. In order to make them bear more fruit, I have to cut them back. God wants us to bear more fruit. As you suffer, you share the comforts of God's Word with those around you. That's bearing fruit. You pray to God more often and more wholeheartedly. That's bearing fruit.

False doctrine can destroy our faith like a disease destroys a berry patch. Maybe you were starting to think God's Word isn't so important. That's a disease. Out of love for you God pruned.

The pruning has changed you. Maybe, for the first time, you find you reach for your Bible daily and have a constant conversation with Jesus in your mind.

"I am the vine; you are the branches. If you remain in me and I in you, you will bear much fruit" (John 15:5).

Life is like a game of Scrabble

Talia Steinhauer

All my Scrabble lovers out there raise your hands; raise them high! My family is obsessed and plays it in person and on our phones. If you know Scrabble, you know the first word on the board is important. Every other word is built off that first word. So you tell me, would you rather start with the word *me* or *Jesus*? The first would give you 8 points, and the next would give 24 points. Also, Jesus offers way more room for growth off the word.

"Therefore everyone who hears these words of mine and puts them into practice is like a wise man who built his house on the rock. The rain came down, the streams rose, and the winds blew and beat against that house; yet it did not fall, because it had its foundation on the rock" (Matthew 7:24,25).

Your foundation is the most important part of your life. What you build everything else on depends on the strength of that foundation. Have you ever heard someone say, "Whatever happens, happens!"? What? I mean, I'm pretty laid-back, but even so, I don't want to rely on myself or on "the universe." I want to know that God is my foundation and that he's got my back no matter what.

Build your foundation on Jesus, knowing that your life can continue to grow stronger and taller. Built on Jesus, you know your foundation can't possibly fall.

Whatever happens, God has a plan to use it for your good. I like that idea way better. Alright, back to my game of Scrabble, both in a godly sense and the app on my phone.

Let there be

Talia Steinhauer

One of my favorite sayings is, "How cool is it that the same God who created mountains and oceans and galaxies looked at you and thought the world needed one of you too." Have you ever really thought about that saying and the magnitude of its meaning for your life?

"And God said, 'Let there be lights in the vault of the sky to separate the day from the night, and let them serve as signs to mark sacred times, and days and years, and let them be lights in the vault of the sky to give light on the earth.' And it was so" (Genesis 1:14,15).

The same God who created all of that with his words knows that you have an important role to play on this earth. Think about all the time and money that we've spent on studying the universe. The same universe that was created by the same God that created you.

So how do we repay God for creating us? We sin. We disrespect him. We deny knowing him. Yet he never stops loving us, because the same God who created the galaxies sent his one and only Son to save us from our sins and bring us to heaven with him.

Take a moment tonight to walk outside and look up at the moon and the stars. Send a prayer of thanks to the God who not only created the universe all around you but created you and cleansed you by the blood of his Son.

It shouldn't make sense

Diana Kerr

"Something is wrong when our lives make sense to unbelievers." I read that sentence, and it struck me hard. Why are we surprised when people don't understand our actions as Christians? If we want to glorify God and not ourselves or the world, shouldn't we honor him no matter how others react?

I have one major regret from college: I lived a safe, watered-down version of my faith. I went to church and never turned away from God, but I lowered my standards so I was just unchristian enough to fit in. Through my words and actions—or lack thereof—I tiptoed around situations I knew were wrong so I didn't stir things up.

First Peter 2:11,12 has a different idea: **"Dear friends, I urge you, as foreigners and exiles, to abstain from sinful desires, which wage war against your soul. Live such good lives among the pagans that, though they accuse you of doing wrong, they may see your good deeds and glorify God on the day he visits us."**

Don't live your life just to fit in or avoid causing waves. Stand up for what you believe in a loving way, even if it's not popular. People will notice. Your God deserves obedience and glory, and there's a world of people all around you who need to come face-to-face with salvation and the truth more than they need your participation in their Christless living.

Here's to living a life that doesn't make sense to unbelievers, in the very best way.

Living a thank-filled life

Tracy Hankwitz

It's easy to be thankful on Thanksgiving Day, but what about every other day?

St. Paul tells us: **"Rejoice always, pray continually, give thanks in all circumstances; for this is God's will for you in Christ Jesus"** (1 Thessalonians 5:16-18).

Wait, what? Give thanks in ALL circumstances? How can I be grateful when the kids are fighting, when facing an overwhelming mountain of bills, when my spouse leaves me, or when I'm told I have cancer?

Jesus has the answer: **"The Lord Jesus, on the night he was betrayed, took bread, and when he had given thanks, he broke it"** (1 Corinthians 11:23,24).

On the night that Judas would betray him, that he would be mocked, beaten, have iron nails pounded through his flesh and hang there on a cross—Jesus gave thanks. He saw the suffering that lay before him as a gift he could give us—one that leads to eternal joy.

The key to being grateful in all things is to see all things as gifts of grace. God's blessings are abundant, even those wrapped in heartache and pain. He uses them all to work his plan for us.

Pray that God will open the eyes of your heart to recognize even the smallest things to be grateful for. Begin to count them, write them down, and you'll soon see that the list of grace gifts is never ending! As you name blessings, you begin to practice the art of thanksgiving, learning to live with a grateful heart.

See all as grace, offer gratitude, and you'll receive joy. This is how to live a thank-filled life.

Rejoice in rejection

Karen Spiegelberg

When my daughters were young and growing rapidly, I took their outgrown clothing to a local consignment shop. I always made sure that everything was in
very good shape. Yet, many times the store would only
keep a few pieces and give me a big thumbs-down on
the others. Then I'd have to endure the walk of shame
as I took the rejected items back to my van. Anyone
who does consignment selling knows the feeling! For
some reason, you don't just feel like your items have
been rejected; you feel rejected personally as well.

Feeling rejected is never a good feeling. But Jesus
called rejection a blessing as he instructed the disciples
in his final days: **"Blessed are you when people hate
you, when they exclude you and insult you and reject
your name as evil, because of the Son of Man. Rejoice in
that day and leap for joy, because great is your reward
in heaven"** (Luke 6:22,23). We are blessed because our
reward is not of this world! And our reward is not of this
world because of the One who gave his life for all who
rejected and hated him. In spite of knowing that and
as a response to that, Jesus further proclaimed, **"Love
your enemies, do good to those who hate you, bless
those who curse you, pray for those who mistreat you"**
(Luke 6:27,28).

Next time my box is rejected by the consignment
store, I'll be reminded that Jesus calls rejection in his
name a blessing and an opportunity. I may even leap for
joy in the parking lot!

The LORD is my strength
and my shield;
my heart trusts in him,
and he helps me.
My heart leaps for joy,
and with my song I praise him.

Psalm 28:7

What joys have made your heart leap this week?
List them here and thank God for them.

_____

_____

_____

_____

_____

_____

That's no cliché

Karen Spiegelberg

What do you think of when someone says, "That's so cliché"? According to the *Oxford English Dictionary*, a *cliché* is "a phrase that is overused and shows no original thought."

Would you ever think that a Bible passage could fit the category of cliché? What about John 3:16, Philippians 4:13, or Romans 8:28—three of the top passages that are quick to be recited or used? "Of course not!" you think. And yet, recently I heard an author whom I respect refer to those passages as cliché. Sigh. They might be used often, but no part of God's Word can be classified as overused or not showing original thought.

Every bit of the Word, the Bible, is equally valuable no matter how often it may or may not be applied. There are plenty of examples to prove it. **"All Scripture is God-breathed and is useful for teaching, rebuking, correcting and training in righteousness"** (2 Timothy 3:16). Did you catch that? All Scripture, not some. Let's go to Romans 15:4: **"Everything that was written in the past was written to teach us, so that through the endurance taught in the Scriptures and the encouragement they provide we might have hope."** Everything that was written. In Matthew 4:4, Jesus himself tells us, **"Man shall not live on bread alone, but on every word that comes from the mouth of God."** Every word from the mouth of God.

And so, **"let the message of Christ dwell in you richly"** (Colossians 3:16). Another well-used passage, but that's no cliché!

Fathers, be good

Diana Kerr

The song "Daughters" by famous musical artist John Mayer has a chorus that says that fathers should be good to their daughters. If they are, their daughters will love like they did. He goes on to say that those daughters, influenced by their parents, become mothers and, therefore, continue the chain of influence on the next generation.

Without a doubt, fathers make an impact on their sons and daughters, especially in their early years. My mom always said that fathers are so influential that most girls end up marrying someone like their dad, for better or worse. I was blessed with a godly, supportive, amazing dad, but I know that isn't the case for everyone.

What legacy did your father leave you? Was he "good to you," as the song "Daughters" says and as God's Word instructs? Or did he leave you with some scars? God provides biblical guidelines for fathers, but sin taints parenthood. Ephesians 6:4 is a classic verse for dads: **"Fathers, do not exasperate your children; instead, bring them up in the training and instruction of the Lord."** Unfortunately, some of us can probably relate more to the first half of that passage than the second half.

So how do we handle Father's Day? First, thank God for your father and for any lessons he taught you, either through positive or negative actions. (If Dad's still around, thank him too.) Second, thank your Father God that he fills in all the gaps where earthly fathers don't always measure up.

Little white lies

Karen Maio

"Does this dress make me look fat?" she asks.

"Absolutely!" he replies.

No man in his right mind would answer that way! Even if the dress didn't flatter her figure, human kindness and tact would keep him from such a response. Thus is born the "little white lie" ("You look great!"), the deceitful fib that is okay because the end (no hurt feelings) justifies the means (being dishonest). Or does it?

Little white lies may seem like no big deal—nobody gets hurt—but once you've told one, it gets easier to tell another. Soon, your integrity is eroded away. You've taught your children that lying is a sin, but they may have caught from your actions that God's law isn't really absolute. And "white"? These sins are far from pure in God's eyes. If left unrepented and willfully reoccurring, they can put your soul in jeopardy. It's no longer no big deal!

Jesus not only taught us about truth; he modeled the truth. While standing bound before Pontius Pilate, he was asked, **"Are you the king of the Jews?"** If ever there was a time for a little white lie! "Uh, no, I'm not a king; I'm their teacher," he could have replied, but he truthfully answered, **"Yes, I am"** (Matthew 27:11 GW).

"Give glory to God by telling the truth" (John 9:24), but be kind and tactful ("I liked the other dress better"). Deceitfulness—even little white lies—is usually found out. It's better to obey God and tell the truth.

Absolutely!

Drink up!

Tracy Hankwitz

Plants need water to grow. This is a basic fact we learn as children and one every gardener knows. Why, then, are there wilting plants in my yard? Why do I wait until they're at the point of death to water them? When I do, it amazes me to see how quickly they perk up.

I see they desperately need water, but why my aversion? Perhaps because my day is full of more important activities: getting the kids up on time, packing lunches, getting myself ready, dealing with job-related issues, watching soccer, preparing a somewhat healthy meal, helping with homework, getting the kids to bed, and then collapsing. When am I supposed to water the plants?

As busy as we are, we are the ones who desperately need life-giving water. Our Master Gardener wants to water us with his refreshing Word of Life. A few minutes spent in his presence studying his Word give us the strength to get through the day. Schedule time with him; make it part of your daily routine. That's how we grow in faith. He says in Jeremiah 17:8, **"They will be like a tree planted by the water that sends out its roots by the stream. It does not fear when heat comes. . . . It has no worries in a year of drought and never fails to bear fruit."**

Busy lives can leave us spiritually wilted without a daily dose of God's Word. As we drink from the stream of life, we are refreshed. When trouble comes, God gives us the strength to bear it because our roots are strong.

So, drink up!

Love, renewal, and hope

Christine Wentzel

It's especially hard to watch our children take foolish and deadly nosedives into darkness before waking up to the life-giving light of Jesus before it's too late. Some are still gone. Some repentantly came back. Through the mercy of second, third, and fourth divine chances, they testify to being pursued by amazing grace.

There's a good example of this pursuit found in the conversion of the apostle Paul. He was thoroughly versed in God's Word. He was taught what the messianic prophecies foretold. He heard the news of their fulfillment through eye witnesses, yet he committed himself to killing the messengers.

They only heard the report: **"'The man who formerly persecuted us is now preaching the faith he once tried to destroy.' And they praised God because of me"** (Galatians 1:23,24).

God could have easily left Paul to his eventual doom. However, his Father wanted his son home. Paul would go on to pursue others for God's kingdom.

No matter how dire it looks for a fool running away from God's true love, the Father is still near him or her. He loves his lost child and leaves reminders for the "blind" one to see. Let us never give up. Ceaselessly pray, and confidently speak the truth in love to that person. It's better to risk losing contact with us than that person lose contact with God.

These kinds of converted "fools" make the best eye witnesses for the rest of us in need of love, renewal, and hope.

Do we have to die?

Talia Steinhauer

Science Talk Question: *Why can't our bodies live forever?* In other words, do we have to die?

I challenge you to discuss this with someone in the next few days. Try talking about it with a Christian and then again with a non-Christian.

We were asked to discuss this in a science class one time in college. I said to my table, "Yeah, that's super interesting, especially because people used to live much longer—like Adam for over nine hundred years." Everyone at my table stared at me as if I had said something insane like there is a God above all gods who sent his perfect Son to the earth to die for my and their misdeeds. THEN he set us right with that holy God in one fell swoop so we will live forever if we believe him!

Oh wait, that's also true! **"I am the resurrection and the life. The one who believes in me will live, even though they die; and whoever lives by believing in me will never die"** (John 11:25,26).

So now with that real happening in mind, how can you discuss this question with unbelievers? Continue to point them to God's Word and explain how it's worked wonders in your life. Give a reason for the hope you carry for admiring and appreciating a God who brought you back to life!

Stand in the light

Carolyn Webb

Have you ever noticed how much difference light makes to how things appear? Sitting in church one morning, I noticed the sunlight reflecting on a warped board in the plank ceiling, but when the sunlight shifted, the problem area was no longer visible. Light makes all the difference in how things look.

The book of John makes many references to Jesus as light. Jesus says of himself, **"I am the light of the world. Whoever follows me will never walk in darkness, but will have the light of life"** (John 8:12). Jesus' light shines on us and shows us where we need to be repaired. Without that light, everything looks just fine and we continue to live as if nothing is wrong. On our own, we see no need for repair, but Jesus' light shows us that we're far from perfect.

The amazing thing is that when God looks at us through that same Jesus light, he doesn't see our imperfections. **"He has reconciled you by Christ's physical body through death to present you holy in his sight, without blemish and free from accusation"** (Colossians 1:22). **"For God did not send his Son into the world to condemn the world, but to save the world through him"** (John 3:17).

Don't shy away from the light for fear of the imperfections you'll see. Stand in the light of Jesus and enjoy the healing power of God's grace and forgiveness.

A true witness

Julie Luetke

I turned to one of my students and told him, "I sprained my ankle this week, and it's all purple. Do you believe me?"

His answer came slowly, "Well, yes, but I'd like to see it."

I took off my shoe and sock and revealed a badly bruised and swollen foot. All of the students quickly said, "I believe; I believe!" As witnesses, they firmly believed.

Jesus did many things to help his disciples believe. He showed them the nail prints in his hands and feet and the mark of the spear in his side. He ate with them, left footprints in the sand, and breathed on them. When he touched them, they felt living bone and muscle. Jesus was preparing his disciples to be his witnesses to the ends of the earth—eye witnesses that would stand up in the courts of people's hearts.

The work Jesus did on earth to live a perfect life for us, take our punishment for sin, and rise to win over death and hell has to be told by witnesses. The disciples are gone, but the words they wrote are not. The Bible is the account of the eye witnesses to an ALIVE Jesus. Only rising from death proves victory over death.

God put the thoughts and the words into the hearts and minds of the writers of the Bible so there would be no mistakes.

"When you received the word of God, which you heard from us, you accepted it not as a human word, but as it actually is, the word of God" (1 Thessalonians 2:13).

Thanks and prayer—
prayer and thanks

Lori Malnes

Recently I've been a little under the weather—nothing bad, just a cold—and my motivation to get anything done has been nonexistent. In my state of "bleh," I was thinking about what I had read recently about prayer and thanksgiving and how the two are intermixed.

I procrastinated by going online and checking out how many times *pray/prayer* and *thanks/thanksgiving* are found coupled in the same sentence in the Bible. Depending on the translation, there are up to 20 such verses sprinkled throughout the Old and New Testaments!

One cool place is in Daniel. After Daniel found out the decree to pray only to King Darius, **"three times a day he got down on his knees and prayed, giving things to his God, just as he had done before"** (Daniel 6:10). Three times a day, every day, Daniel prayed and gave thanks to God—prayer and thanks together—no matter what.

Then in Philippians 4:6, Paul tells us, **"Do not be anxious about anything, but in every situation, by prayer and petition, with thanksgiving, present your requests to God."** With thanksgiving—in every situation—we are to come before God in prayer and with thanksgiving.

I think I go about my days far too often without even seeing or appreciating the little things, all the little blessings that God gives me each and every day. If I don't notice the little things, I might miss the big things as well. May I do as Colossians 4:2 says, **"Devote yourselves to prayer, being watchful and thankful."** Prayer and thanks.

"I want him to be in heaven"
Erica Koester

A couple years ago, a missionary showed up at our door. My husband engaged him in conversation for two hours. They discussed their differing religions on a bi-weekly basis until we moved, and they still communicate via email to this day. At some point in this process, I asked my husband, "What is the point of spending so much time witnessing to him?" Not missing a beat, my husband responded, "I want him to be in heaven." It hit me like a ton of bricks. Over time, I had drawn my own flawed, human conclusion that this man would simply never come to faith.

Thankfully, God's promise to us concerning this matter is far more gracious: **"As the rain and the snow come down from heaven, and do not return to it without watering the earth . . . so is my word that goes out from my mouth: It will not return to me empty, but will accomplish what I desire and achieve the purpose for which I sent it"** (Isaiah 55:10,11).

This is really good news for any of us who dearly love unbelievers. God loves them even more dearly, and he can work a miracle in their hearts! This passage is also an encouraging call to action. Speak the truth in love to that coworker, cousin, or neighbor. These may be some of the most difficult conversations we ever have, but I can't think of any conversation more important. God will bless your words, and he wants that precious soul in heaven even more than we do.

It's time to cheer!

Janet Gehlhar

Easter morning is thrilling. We rejoice and sing, "Alleluia!" because we're celebrating Jesus' victory over sin and Satan.

"'He is not here; he has risen! Remember how he told you, while he was still with you in Galilee: "The Son of Man must be delivered into the hands of sinners, be crucified and on the third day be raised again."' Then they remembered his words" (Luke 24:6-8).

I try to imagine myself as one of the women who went to the grave early Easter morning filled with sorrow and bewilderment. Arriving to find the stone rolled away and an empty tomb must have been overwhelming in their state of grief. And then, to see an angel and to hear him say that Jesus has risen! The angel reminded them what they already knew but had forgotten. Jesus had told them that on the third day he would rise. Oh yeah—that makes sense now. The shock at this turn of events must have sent their heads spinning. Their deep grief was changed to extreme joy and amazement that Jesus was alive.

God is all powerful, and Easter is another example of his supremacy. Jesus paid the penalty for our sins on the cross, and by his resurrection, he showed that we too can look forward to eternity in heaven. How humbling to think that this same God is the one who loves you and me, forgives us, and has a place in heaven waiting for us.

I'm going to sing the Easter hymns with gusto because my thankfulness can't be held in.

New and exciting!

Karen Maio

It's that time of year again—fresh boxes of crayons, pages of empty notebooks, the latest pop culture character emblazoned on backpacks. School is back in session!

Sigh. So why do I feel like I have the post-Christmas (or wedding or performance) "blahs"? The only new thing on my plate is a construction-riddled school route during peak traffic hours. Ugh! Time to turn to the Word!

A search of the word *new* had this Bible passage speaking to my heart: **"Put off your old self, which is being corrupted by its deceitful desires; to be made new in the attitude of your minds; and to put on the new self, created to be like God in true righteousness and holiness"** (Ephesians 4:22-24).

God wants us to change actively the behavior of our old self, our sinful nature. With the Holy Spirit's help, our conduct will change and our attitudes will too. **"For we are God's handiwork, created in Christ Jesus to do good works, which God prepared in advance for us to do"** (Ephesians 2:10).

We put on the new self, the way God created us to be—holy and righteous. Jesus was crucified for our sins and now, through faith in him as our Savior, his righteousness becomes our new clothing! Out of love for everything our Savior has done for us and our salvation, we want to change, put on the new self, and become more Christ-like!

It's amazing how being in the Word can chase any blahs away. God has pointed out that I do have something new. I have a whole new self! How exciting!

Silver crowns
Christine Wentzel

"Silver hair is a beautiful crown found in a righteous life" (Proverbs 16:31 GW).

Mature women may not consider their silver hair the result of righteousness. It seems to come from genetics, stress, iffy health, and old age. However, what God means is that a long life lived in his name has great reward. When a life is lived long enough for hair to turn white, people are more than accustomed to the trials and fears that tested their faith through the years.

That's where the reward begins to pay dividends. Older sisters in Christ are blessed with several decades of experience under their belts; it's a valuable treasure to pass on. Delight in this knowledge gained from your weaknesses and God's strength. Don't hesitate to share it.

May the confidence and peace of these women be an engaging and attractive magnet for the younger sisters in Christ to seek their wisdom. May these older peers take the younger under their wings to encourage them through school, marriage, parenthood, and careers. These young lives are inquisitive, fearless, and anxious. The reward they give their mentors puts a purposeful step in a faith walk that sometimes appears no longer to serve a holy purpose.

Straighten those crowns, dear princesses of the King. There's work to do!

Fans in heaven

Julie Luetke

Have you ever lost your voice because you cheered so loudly? Have your hands stung from clapping? Have you been so excited about the game that you didn't notice the snow in the air and the biting wind? You probably remember it with a smile. The team never asked you to cheer yourself silly. You wanted to; you couldn't help it!

Being a fan is not boring when your team wins. It's especially exciting when the fight to win takes real skill and determination. The harder it is to win, the louder we cheer. Satan was no pushover. The temptations of the devil were real. If not for Jesus' win over death, we would have no hope of life eternal in heaven. Jesus is a true MVP.

We like to think of our team as winning for us. Jesus really did win for us. By willingly going to a cross in our place and rising from the dead, Jesus won! It was a solid win over sin and death. No playoff needed. It is finished.

"Then I heard every creature in heaven and on earth and under the earth and on the sea, and all that is in them, saying: 'To him who sits on the throne and to the Lamb be praise and honor and glory and power, for ever and ever!'" (Revelation 5:13).

P.S. MVP stands for My Victorious Prince of Peace.

New year, new start

Carolyn Webb

Do you make New Year's resolutions? Typically, my resolutions don't look much different from the average American's and fall within the top five resolutions: (1) lose weight, (2) get organized, (3) spend less; save more, (4) enjoy life to the fullest, (5) stay fit and healthy.

This year I resolved to adjust my attitude. In reflecting on the past year, I found myself fostering a negative attitude about many things. While New Year's resolutions don't have a biblical origin, there are Bible passages that are applicable to making a new start. To guide my attitude adjustment, I selected a few Bible passages.

Each day is a chance to start over:

"Because of the LORD's great love we are not consumed, for his compassions never fail. They are new every morning; great is your faithfulness" (Lamentations 3:22,23).

Don't let the past get in the way of the future:

"But one thing I do: Forgetting what is behind and straining toward what is ahead, I press on toward the goal to win the prize for which God has called me heavenward in Christ Jesus" (Philippians 3:13,14).

Be thankful for God's blessings:

"Give thanks to the LORD, for he is good; his love endures forever" (Psalm 118:1).

Whether you make resolutions or not, may God bless your new year and give you a peaceful, thankful heart.

When the going gets tough

April Cooper

The weather here has been quite sunny lately, with mild temperatures for this time of year. But after several nice weather days in a row, unexpected rain has now set in. Not a light mist or drizzle but a hard rain with drops that hit the windshield with force. And the forecast now has clouds and rain for the next few days—straight in a row.

Isn't that just like life sometimes? All is going well, routines are in place, and seemingly everything is going just as it should. Then, without warning, a crisis or trial appears, bringing the sense of serenity to an abrupt halt. It seems to catch us by surprise, but should it? Life can seem just like the weather, unpredictable!

Scripture teaches us in John 16:33: **"I have told you these things, so that in me you may have peace. In this world you will have trouble. But take heart! I have overcome the world."** This verse assures us that hard times, challenges, and trials will indeed come to our doorsteps. But it also assures us that peace in Christ Jesus is given even in the midst of it all.

Remember the words of John 16:33, rest in God's promises, and keep a positive attitude during those hard times. It can make all the difference in how you get through problems that arise.

You have been chosen

Diana Kerr

My family is unapologetically in love with all the *Toy Story* movies. (My mom cheered, clapped, and cried in the theater during *Toy Story 2*.) Remember the first movie when Buzz and Woody end up inside a claw machine at the arcade and Sid picks them up with the claw? "He has been chosen! He has been chosen!" all the toy aliens left behind inside the machine repeat. They're totally psyched for Woody and Buzz; being "chosen" is a big deal.

You can probably guess where I'm headed with this. You and I are chosen too, but by our gracious God, not some kid at an arcade. Most of the time, though, we have identity amnesia, and that's a problem. See, 1 Peter 2:9 says, **"You are a chosen people, a royal priesthood, a holy nation, God's special possession, that you may declare the praises of him who called you out of darkness into his wonderful light."**

Chosen. Royal. Holy. God's special possession. This is what we are. One of the problems when we forget this lies in the second half of the verse. We were meant to declare God's praises, but we obviously don't do this much when we forget our identity.

Read the verse again and let it soak in. Your identity is incredible and wonderful, and you have done nothing to deserve that. You have been chosen and redeemed by a God who's crazy about you. Own that identity, acknowledge the gift that it is, and go praise God publicly.

A father's love

Karen Spiegelberg

On Father's Day each year we celebrate dads. That day is bittersweet for me since my own went home to heaven. But whether you've had a great dad in your life or someone who has fit that role, there's something special about that love for us as girls and women. A great dad will love you unconditionally through your childhood tantrums, your first car accident, and your bad choices of boyfriends. He will show patience as you grow into the adult God will have you be, and he will be there whenever you need him. How great is the love of a father!

First John 3:1 tells us, **"See what great love the Father has lavished on us, that we should be called children of God! And that is what we are!"**

Our heavenly Father and his love are even more precious than an earthly father! He forgives the tantrums and poor choices and uses them for our good and to his glory. He is not only there whenever we need him, but he has done the ultimate that any father could do—sacrificed his own Son for the sins and sake of us, his own precious children. Because of that, we will have eternal life and live at "home" with him and in his presence forever.

My own dad now enjoys that reward. He is at home with his Father and my Father. What a beautiful thing to imagine. I think next Father's Day will not be bittersweet; it will be very sweet.

My Prayer List

Therefore, since we have a great high priest who has ascended into heaven, Jesus the Son of God, let us hold firmly to the faith we profess. For we do not have a high priest who is unable to empathize with our weaknesses, but we have one who has been tempted in every way, just as we are—yet he did not sin. Let us then approach God's throne of grace with confidence, so that we may receive mercy and find grace to help us in our time of need.

Hebrews 4:14-16

Date: **Praying for:**

_____   _____

_____   _____

_____   _____

_____   _____

_____   _____

_____   _____

_____   _____

_____   _____

_____   _____

Date: **Praying for:**

My Worship Service and Bible Study Reflections

*Then he opened their minds so
they could understand the Scriptures.*

Luke 24:45

Use these pages to capture the insights gained from
God's Word during times of worship and study.

Date: _____

_____

_____

_____

_____

_____

Date: _____

_____

_____

_____

_____

_____

Date: _____

_____

_____

_____

_____

_____

Date: _____

_____

_____

_____

_____

_____

Date: _____

_____

_____

_____

_____

_____

Date: _____

_____

_____

_____

_____

_____

Date: _____

_____

_____

_____

_____

_____

Date: _____

_____

_____

_____

_____

_____

Date: _____

_____

_____

_____

_____

_____

Date: _____

_____

_____

_____

_____

_____

Date: _____

_____

_____

_____

_____

_____

Topical Index

God's Character: 13, 15, 17, 19, 21, 24, 32, 38, 47, 60, 81, 95, 110, 112, 130, 142, 143, 146, 153, 177, 184, 196

Faith/Hope: 34, 46, 52, 56, 94, 126, 174, 202

Prayer-filled Living: 66, 125, 140, 144, 170, 198

Salvation/Renewal: 12, 22, 23, 35, 45, 75, 84, 137, 195, 203, 206

Seasons/Holidays: 26, 39, 40, 86, 154, 181, 186, 191, 201, 204, 207

Sin/Brokenness: 37, 67, 85, 93, 96, 103, 116, 118, 119, 122, 127, 134, 136, 138, 145, 150, 160, 162, 166, 173, 176, 179, 192

Spiritual Growth: 11, 14, 18, 20, 30, 31, 41, 44, 53, 61, 63, 64, 70, 71, 73, 74, 76, 77, 78, 79, 80, 83, 90, 98, 99, 100, 105, 106, 107, 111, 113, 120, 133, 135, 141, 151, 159, 161, 164, 165, 171, 182, 185

Thank-filled Living: 10, 16, 25, 167, 172, 200

Trials/Temptations: 55, 57, 58, 82, 87, 115, 131, 132, 152, 156, 157, 163, 187, 205

Trust: 36, 43, 50, 51, 54, 59, 72, 91, 102, 104, 123, 147, 158

Wisdom/Bible: 27, 33, 42, 92, 97, 101, 121, 155, 175, 178, 180, 183, 190, 193

Witnessing: 62, 65, 114, 117, 124, 139, 194, 197, 199

Seasonal Bible Reading Plan

(Some with applicable devotions)

Spring (March/April)

2 Corinthians 5:20-6:2
(116)

Psalm 51

Genesis 2:7-9,15-17; 3:1-7
(180)

Romans 5:12-19
(15, 52, 58, 163)

Genesis 12:1-8

John 4:5-26
(40, 126)

John 9:1-7,13-17,34-39
(192)

Psalm 143

Hosea 5:15-6:3
(140)

Romans 8:1-10,11-19
(190)

Matthew 20:17-28

Psalms 42 and 43

John 11:17-27,38-45
(38, 100, 195)

Eastertime (April/May)

Hebrews 4:14-16; 5:7-9
(37, 133, 178)

John 13:1-15,34

Isaiah 52:13-53:12

Zechariah 9:9,10

Philippians 2:5-11
(70, 77)

Matthew 21:1-11

Psalm 24
(41)

Isaiah 12:1-6

1 Corinthians 15:51-57
(18, 46, 85, 162)

John 20:1-18

Psalm 30
(12)

Psalm 118
(98, 204)

Acts 2:14,36-47

Luke 24:13-35

1 Peter 2:4-10,19-25
(17, 104, 115, 206)

John 10:1-10
(71, 170)

Psalm 23
(102)

John 14:1-12
(26)

1 Peter 3:15-22
(38, 70)

Psalm 66

Acts 1:1-11

1 Peter 4:12-17; 5:6-11
(61, 159)

Summer (June-September)

John 16:5-11
(63, 155, 205)

Genesis 1:1–2:3
(180, 184)

Matthew 28:16-20
(90, 97, 145)

Romans 3:21-25,27,28

Matthew 9:9-13
(157)

Romans 5:6-11
(15, 52, 58, 163)

Matthew 9:35-10:8

Psalm 100
(56)

Romans 6:1-11

Romans 7:15-25
(82)

Matthew 11:25-30
(120)

Psalm 145
(91)

Isaiah 55:10,11
(101, 112, 199)

Romans 8:18-25

Romans 8:28-30
(190)

Romans 8:35-39

Matthew 14:13-33
(36, 57, 106)

Psalms 42-43

Psalm 73
(51)

Matthew 15:21-28
(132)

Psalms 133 and 134

Psalm 34
(14, 107, 145)

Autumn (September-November)

Matthew 16:21-26

Romans 13:1-10

Matthew 18:15-35
(165, 179)

Genesis 50:15-21

Psalm 27

Philippians 3:12-21
(18, 204)

Philippians 4:4-13
(31, 34, 144, 172, 190, 198)

Matthew 22:34-46

Matthew 25:14-46
(114)

Matthew 10:16-23

Psalm 46

1 Thessalonians 5:1-11
(151)

Christmastime (December)

Romans 13:11-14

Romans 15:4-13
(123, 190)

Matthew 1:18-25
(19)

Isaiah 9:2-7

John 1:1-14
(45)

Psalm 98

Ephesians 1:3-6,15-18
(23, 26, 93, 137, 157)

Winter (January/February)

Isaiah 49:1-6,13-18
(12, 25)

Matthew 5:1-12

Matthew 5:13-20

Matthew 5:21-37
(113)

Psalm 103
(140)

Matthew 6:24-34
(47, 137, 181)

2 Peter 1:16-21

Meet the Authors

Karen Spiegelberg lives in Wisconsin with her husband, Jim. She has three married daughters, two grandsons, and has been a foster mom to many. Years ago she was encouraged to start a women's ministry but was unsure of the timing. When her brother died suddenly, it hit her hard—that we can't wait until the time seems right for ministry; the time is now. And so in 2009, with God's direction, *A Word for Women* was born. Karen finds great encouragement in Psalm 31:14,15: "But I trust in you, O Lord. . . . My times are in your hands." www.awordforwomen.com

Christine Wentzel is a native of Milwaukee but lives in Norfolk, Virginia, with her husband, James, and their rescued fur-children. After two lost decades as a prodigal, Christine gratefully worships and serves her Salvation Winner at Resurrection Church in Chesapeake, Virginia. There she discovered latent talents to put to use for her holy King. In 2009 she began to write and create graphic design for *A Word for Women,* which eventually led to becoming its coadministrator as well. She is determined to speak with a frank, balanced view on the impact of our God-given free will.

April Cooper is married to Davis and is the proud mom of four children. By day, she is a virtual teacher. In her spare time, she enjoys writing and photography and continues to improve her American Sign Language skills. She believes that all aspects of the Christian life should be lived in a way that glorifies God. Visit April at her book website—*When the Tide Is Low* (www.authoraprilcooper.com)—and her nonprofit ministry—Lavender, Lilac and Lilies (www.gardeninspiration.org).

Janet Gehlhar lives in Hager City, Wisconsin, with her husband, Jeff. They have three grown daughters. She leads the women's ministry at St. John's Church in Red Wing, Minnesota. Her prayer is to be God's tool to help others grow in their faith and trust in him. She strives to always trust God's way—especially when it doesn't seem to make sense at the moment. Her favorite Bible verse is Isaiah 55:8: "'For my thoughts are not your thoughts, neither are your ways my ways,' declares the Lord."

Tracy Hankwitz is a proud mama of four, a horticulturist by day, and a beauty seeker for life. She is a Word lover and wanna-be photographer, dwelling in possibilities and striving to live a grateful life. She and her husband have a bit of earth in Wisconsin where she gardens, juggles life, and blogs about discovering God's grace in all things. Her love for nature, music, and photography is woven into her encouraging devotions at www.idwellinpossibilities.wordpress.com.

Diana Kerr lives in Milwaukee, Wisconsin, with her husband, Kyle, and their son, Harrington. She is a certified professional life coach on a mission to help go-getter Christian women break free from overwhelm and design their time and lives for what matters most. Visit www.dianakerr.com to learn more about working with Diana and explore her free tips and resources on intentional living.

Erica Koester is a wife to Paul (a pastor and college dorm supervisor); mom to one-year old William; and owner of a tiny, fluffy dog named Reggie. They reside in New Ulm, Minnesota, and greatly enjoy spending time with family and friends. Erica works in client services for a large sci-

entific research company. Her favorite Bible section is a tie between Hebrews 11:1–12:1-3 and the book of Philippians. She hopes that her devotions lead you to realize God's incredible goodness and faithfulness.

Julie Luetke lives in Watertown, Wisconsin, with her retired pastor husband, Joel. She is a wife, mother, and grandmother. She is also a quilter, gardener, and volunteer with Jesus Cares Ministries, www.tlha.org/jesus-cares-ministries. Her favorite title is Daughter of the King.

Karen Maio, her husband, and son spend time in Milwaukee and Eagle River, Wisconsin. She is a former certified public accountant (rheumatoid arthritis sidetracked her professional career). She currently enjoys being a mom, composer, devotion writer, and community theater actress. You can find her songs at www.nph.net. She hopes her words—centered on his Word—encourage you as you walk with Christ. "Trust in the LORD with all your heart and lean not on your own understanding" (Proverbs 3:5).

Lori Malnes and her husband, Dave, hail from the evangelism-training ministry www.PraiseandProclaim.com. They have 4 + 1 (son-in-law) adult children and 3 grandchildren. Lori writes, "He is everywhere and in everything I do—He is IN me and I in him." One of her favorite verses is Psalm 19:14: "May these words of my mouth and this meditation of my heart be pleasing in your sight, O LORD, my Rock and my Redeemer."

Talia Steinhauer lives her passion as a second-grade teacher in a Christian elementary school. She loves encouraging her students in their faith and is amazed at her faith growth through these interactions. Much of her

writing inspiration comes from the childlike faith she sees in her students. Talia and her husband, Alex, live in southern Wisconsin, where they enjoy hiking, golfing, and trying out as many fish fries as possible. "Let us run with perseverance the race marked out for us" (Hebrews 12:1).

Carolyn Webb lives in Brookfield, Wisconsin, with her husband, Brian; dog, Fritz; and cat, Cricket, and attends Christ the Lord Church. She is a mom of two grown children and a manager of a hospital laboratory. Carolyn writes from her own daily struggles to live as God's child in a less than godly world. She holds tight to her confirmation verse: "Be strong and courageous. Do not be afraid; do not be discouraged, for the LORD your God will be with you wherever you go" (Joshua 1:9).

About Time of Grace

Time of Grace connects people to God's grace—his love, glory, and power—so they realize the temporary things of life don't satisfy. What brings satisfaction is knowing that because Jesus lived, died, and rose for all of us, we have access to the eternal God—right now and forever.

To discover more, please visit timeofgrace.org or call 800.661.3311.

Help share God's message of grace!

Every gift you give helps Time of Grace reach people around the world with the good news of Jesus. Your generosity and prayer support take the gospel of grace to others through our ministry outreach and help them experience a satisfied life as they see God all around them.

Give today at timeofgrace.org/give or by calling 800.661.3311.

Thank you!

Made in the USA
Monee, IL
21 March 2020

23630788R00125